REALISM & OTHER ILLUSIONS:
ESSAYS ON THE CRAFT OF FICTION

Thomas E. Kennedy

Wordcraft of Oregon
2002

By Thomas E. Kennedy

FICTION

Crossing Borders (1990)
Weather of the Eye (1996)
Unreal City (1996)
The Book of Angels (1997)
Drive, Dive, Dance & Fight (1997)

NONFICTION

Andre Dubus: A Study of the Short Fiction (1988)
Robert Coover: A Study of the Short Fiction (1992)
Index to American Award Stories, 1970 -90 (1993)
Realism & Other Illusions: Essays (2002)

ANTHOLOGIES: EDITOR

New Danish Fiction: Special issue of The Review of
        Contemporary Fiction, with Frank Hugus (1995)
New Irish Writing: Special issue of The Literary Review (1997)
The American Short Story Today (1991)
Poems & Sources:Special issue of The Literary Review (1998)
Stories & Sources: Special issue of The Literary Review (2000)
The Secret Life of Writers, with Walter Cummins: Special issue
        of The Literary Review, (2002)

CROSSING BORDERS

"Kennedy makes a stunning debut as a novelist here in this uncannily accurate and beautifully controlled anatomy of a contemporary marital malaise as ubiquitous as the common cold. I shudder to think what it cost his soul to write this."

– Jack Myers, author of *As Long As You're Happy*

"...shimmering with emotional honesty..."
— *New York Times Book Review*

WEATHER OF THE EYE

"Kennedy is a writer of great discernment and a clear sense of what is to be valued. He has the courage to look for our connections with the transcendent."

– Gladys Swan, author of *Carnival of the Gods*

"...a powerful novella of a father's death. Kennedy writes with great command and great perception of this crossroads moment in almost everyone's life."

– Robie Macauley

UNREAL CITY

"Thomas E. Kennedy's fiction has won him a devoted band of followers who know what the rest of the literary world is just finding out: that he's writing some of the most intelligent and beautifully crafted short fiction in America...fresh and contemporary and very much his own."

– W.D. Wetherell, author of *Chekhov's Sister*

"...Kennedy has chosen to create beautiful gems of the imagination in a world which is increasingly wooed and seduced by tawdry, cheap imitations and reproductions."

– Alan Hibbard in *Rain Taxi*

THE BOOK OF ANGELS

"Kennedy's *The Book of Angels* is that rare beast, a novel that boasts both tight plotting and suspense-laden narrative with style and literary profundity. A novel about imagination and will. *The Book of Angels* will delight both readers of the fantastic as well as those who seek more in fiction, a *tour de force* that transcends its raw materials."

    – Gordon Weaver, author of *Cadence*

"...leaves the reader gasping for breath..."

    – *Kansas City Star*

DRIVE, DRIVE, DANCE & FIGHT

"Intense, humorous, sexually charged, emotionally powerful, the stories in Thomas E. Kennedy's *Drive, Dive, Dance & Fight* brilliantly mine the hidden recesses of the human heart. Kennedy is a dazzling writer, literary, compelling and profound."

    – Duff Brenna, author of *The Book of Mamie* & *Too Cool*

"Kennedy writes with wisdom and it is perhaps that wisdom which turns some of his stories of great sorrow into something triumphant. His stories are as good as any I've been reading in the past 10 years or more."

    – Andre Dubus II

"Kennedy's stories pulse with humor, moral edge and a deep sympathy for the human predicament. His fiction comes as a gift from across the sea of a fine writer's untamed imagination."

– James Carroll, author of *Constantine's Sword, American Requiem, Mortal Friends*

REALISM & OTHER ILLUSIONS:
ESSAYS ON THE CRAFT OF FICTION

Thomas E. Kennedy

The content of this book has been adapted and developed from pieces originally published in: *Agni, AWP Chronicle/Writers Chronicle, American Book Review, American Poetry Review, Best Writing on Writing, Chariton Review, Glimmer Train, Green Mountains Review, Hollins Critic, Kenyon Review, The Literary Review, Literary Review of Canada, New Letters, New Novel Review, Newsletter of the Nordic Association of American Studies, New Writers Magazine, Poets & Writers, Potpourri, Quarterly West, Revue Delta, Sewanee Review, Seattle Review, The Writer, The Writers Handbook, Write Magazine, Writers Ask, Writers Forum (Colorado), Writers Forum (UK)*

The short story "What Does God Care About Your Dignity, Victor Travesti?" appeared originally in *New Letters* magazine, University of Missouri-Kansas City, Vol. 55, No. 3, Spring 1989. It was subsequently reprinted in *The Whole Story* (Bench Press, Columbia, S.C:, 1996), *The Literary Review, Stories & Sources* (Vol 41 No 1, Fall 1998) and was included in the collection *Unreal City* (Wordcraft of Oregon, 1996).

The short story "Dust" appeared originally in *New Delta Review* (Vol 8, No 1, Summer 1992) and was reprinted in *Drive, Dive, Dance & Fight* (BkMk Press of University of Missouri-Kansas City, 1997.)

The metafiction, "Noses in Fiction," appeared originally in *New Novel Review*, Vol. 4, No. 1, (Fall 1996), guest edited by Ben Stoltzfus, Univ. of California, Riverside, published by Elmira College, Elmira, NY

"Oh that my words
were now written!
Oh that they were
printed in a book!"
  – Job 19:23

"Life is short, art long, opportunity
fleeting, experiment perilous,
judgement difficult."
  -Hippocrates

"Above all stupdendous inventions, what eminence
of mind was his who dreamed of finding means to
communicate his deepest thoughts to any other
person, no matter how far distant in place and
time? Of speaking with those who are in India,
of speaking with those who are not yet born and
will not be born for a thousand or ten thousand
years? And with what facility? All by using the
various arrangements of twenty little characters
on a page!"
  -Gallileo (quoted by Italo Calvino in
  Six Memos for the Next Millennium
  (tr William Weaver)

I would like to express warm thanks to Drue Heinz and the directors and staff of her Hawthornden Castle who fed, sheltered, and comforted me in the winter of 2000, enabling me to complete this book.

This book is dedicated to the colleagues in this art with whom I have had the privilege to teach, from whom I have had the good fortune to learn, and for whom I feel deep admiration and friendship:

Gordon Weaver, Duff Brenna, Andre Dubus II, Andre Dubus III, Walter Cummins, W. D. Wetherell, Robie Macauley, David Applefield, Pamela Painter, Barry Brent, Askold Melnyczuk, Alexandra Johnson, Alexandra Marshall, James Carroll, Robert Stewart, James McKinley, Lance Olsen, Susan Schwartz Senstad, Greg Herriges, David Memmott, Gladys Swan, Rick Mulkey, Susan Tekulve, Susan Tiberghien, Paul Casey, Dennis Bormann, Claire Bateman, Jack Myers, Carol Allen, Nick Carbo, Denise Duhamel, Isabel Huggan, Sharon Sheehe Stark, Jean Hollander, Peter Meinke, Rosa Shand, Wallis Wilde Menozzi, John Jenkins, Paul Wadden, Julie Fay, Jodi Varon, Lauren Davis, Alan Hibbard, Susan M. Dodd, Polly Swafford, Herman Swafford, Richard Hoffman

With a particular word of thanks to David Memmott for his warm and generous encouragement and support over the past many years.

To Alice who always listens

and always, to Daniel and Isabel

CONTENTS

9

Preface

Although I hope this book might be of interest to other writers, prospective writers, and serious readers of fiction curious about the processes, it is not intended as a how-to.

Rather, it is a collection of my own thoughts and meditations gathered from four decades of writing, studying, and teaching the art of writing, talking about writing with students and writer friends, writing about writing, reading about writing, and practising writing as the nearest thing I have to a spiritual discipline.

My first attempt to write a story was when I was eight and my father brought home a gleaming black Remington manual which was so state of the art you could flip a switch to elevate the ribbon and make it print red. It also had a shift lock so you could free your ten fingers to type all caps. On such a machine, I thought, a boy could easy write a book. My plan was to type the climactic scene in all caps red. As the book was to be about a priest huddled in a cave awaiting his martyrdom at the hands of unholy savages, I thought this a neat touch. I was in third grade at Saint Bartholomew's School and Sister Mary Magdalene had been feeding us stories of missionary priests tortured to death by the Indians of the Americas so I guess I assumed there was a market for such tales.

However, I had not reckoned on the grueling physical effort of hunting and punching even a single paragraph. After quite some time, that was all I had, and I was exhausted, and dinner was ready, so I flicked to red, shift-locked, and typed:

BUT HE THANKED HIS GOD AS THE SAVAGES ENTERED THE CAVE TO KILL HIM FOR HE KNEW HE WAS DYING FOR CHRIST! THE END.

So exhausted was I that nearly ten years would pass before I seriously thought of trying again; I was in junior year in highschool then and had just learned touch-typing, the same year I read Dostoevski, Camus, Gide, Huxley, Steinbeck, and Katherine Mansfield. Her story "Miss Brill" produced a fury in me for I held Ms. Mansfield personally responsible for the pain she had caused this same poor Miss Brill as an object of cruel derision. I intended to send her an irate letter, chastizing her soundly for this until I learned, studying the biographical note on the book, that she had been dead for some forty years. It seemed then as though she had reached across the very chasm of death and decades to touch deep into my seventeen year old heart. A very neat trick which I thought I would like to learn myself.

Twenty years would pass of more or less consistent trying between that night and my first real publication - a short story very unlike "Miss Brill" entitled "The Sins of Generals," which Martin Tucker paid me twenty dollars to publish in *Confrontation*. A breakthrough of sorts. In the next twenty years, I would publish more than a dozen books, nearly a hundred stories and twice as many poems, essays, translations, and other articles.

Although that first twenty years was a time of extreme frustration, it did teach me an essential lesson: that the joy must be in the writing itself or it's not worth a thing. There are any number of trades at which you can make good money and which leave you cold and hungry. Writing is the only one I know that brings its own warmth and sustenance.

I. ESSAYS ON CRAFT & ASSOCIATED MATTERS

CAN YOU LEARN TO WRITE? "I NEVER HAD TO."

As I write this, I sit in the Bronte room of Hawthornden, a medievel castle on a secluded crag overlooking the valley of the river North Esk. Here I shall be for the coming days, preparing this book for print, and here the great Ben Jonson was also once the guest of William Drummond, who owned the castle. Thus, it seems appropriate — even if Jonson and Drummond parted on less than friendly terms at that time — to begin this work with a quote from Dr. Jonson: "A good poet is made as well as born."

I do not believe there has ever been a successful writer who has not studied writing to learn the craft. Here perhaps we must define terms, to wit "successful" and "studied." I shall eschew any attempt to define the former lest I find myself vulnerable to charges of having excluded features from the profile of success simply because they are not mine own (e.g., an appearance on Oprah Winfrey, publication by a major New York house, front-face displays in airports and Barnes & Noble, rave reviews in the *New York Times Book Review*, and so forth). Granted, these and other attributes might accompany the highest literary excellence, but these are not the measures of success to which I refer, which I can most simply identify as writing that is in some manner a profound expression of our existential predicament; in the words of another local Scot, from just eight miles down the road in Edinburgh, Robert Louis Stevenson:

> "The poet...is to find some way of speaking about life that shall satisfy, if only for the moment, (wo)man's enduring astonishment at his(her) own position. And besides having an answer ready, it

is he who shall provoke the question. He must shake people out of their indifference, and force them to make some election in this world, instead of sliding dully forward in a dream... He is the declared enemy of all living by reflex action, of all that is done betwixt sleep and waking, of all the pleasureless pleasurings and imaginary duties in which we coin away our hearts and fritter invaluable years."

I believe that any writer whose work can be thus described would have had to study writing. Reading and contemplating the work of the masters is the classic manner of doing so. A writer may do this on his or her own, in isolation, and/or by building and judiciously using a network of intelligent colleagues, and/or by pursuing a course of formal study of literature and/or the art of writing.

In brief, one can do it alone, on one's own, or one can do it in community with others. I have tried it both ways and find the latter method far superior to the former.

Some writers — even some who make their living teaching college writing courses — pride themselves on saying, "I never took a course in writing. I never had to." Others — for example, the extremely gifted fiction writer W. D. Wetherell — never took a writing course or even met another writer until some time into their careers, but do not make a point of honor of this.

Wetherell worked in isolation for some years before joining the faculty of Vermont College's MFA Program. He likened the moment of being welcomed by fellow faculty member Gordon Weaver his first day there to the historic meeting in the wilderness between H. M. Stanley and David Livingstone (another Scot whose statue stands alongside the enormous monument to Sir Walter Scott on Princes Street in Edinburgh):

"Professor Weaver, I presume."

Writing in isolation, Wetherell had published two books and many stories (and has gone on to publish many more), but had never met another writer before that moment. However, that he had never taken a writing course is not the same as saying he had never studied writing; clearly, he had — he had studied and learned from the masters he most admired; Hawthorne, Melville, Proust, Chekhov...

I am not certain that all potential writers are capable, given the limited years alloted us, of learning the craft they need on their own just as most people would be hard pressed to build a house without first being taught a few things about brick and timber, shingle and cement, without at least studying how a few sturdy houses have been put together, without examining the way a door is hung, a lintel set in place, windows cast, how to pitch and raise a roof, angle the walls, lay flooring, not to mention seeing to the electricity, plumbing, heat ducts...

Never having studied such matters a person might succeed, on superficial observation and surmisal, in constructing some semblance of a house, but not likely one that stands straight and flush, with doors that shut tightly, free of drafts and secure against the weather. A novel written in similar ignorance is more than likely to be subject to similar flaws — a lopsided, insecure structure that offers little shelter and is liable to collapse on your head at any moment.

When I was starting out, I took what undergraduate courses were available to me. My first help was the advice of my freshman college composition professor at C.C.N.Y. to keep a journal in order to loosen up my style and to try to write something in it every day, even if only a single sentence. "And then," he said, "in a year or two, who knows? You might even have a book." Good bait for me. I was seventeen, and four years of keeping a journal — sometimes just a sentence or two, sometimes many pages, sometimes with gaps of weeks or even months — did indeed get me in the habit of writing and writing freely. To learn to write freely is important.

Next I took a course with Edward Hoagland which included individual writing conferences, maybe four or five twenty-minute

17

sessions. These brief meetings resulted in major progress. That was after a few years wandering alone in the wilderness, so to speak, hitch hiking around the United States in the mid-sixties as I thought Jack Kerouac would have wanted me to do, scribbling in my journals (which I carried around in an attaché case ultimately stolen from me in San Francisco — I cannot help but pity the poor junky when he discovered the contents of the alluring stolen case, pages of ringbound scribble.)

What Hoagland did in conference was essentially a commented line-editing. I had learned from my journals to write freely; I was helped by him to rein it in, slice away the excess. I sat beside him and watched him run his pen over my lines, crossing out words, phrases, sentences, saying things like, "You are including *every fucking detail!*" That single statement broke ice for me because I was ready for it. "This is purple prose," he said another time about a piece I had thought lucious as Dylan Thomas's fiction. "Horribly overwritten." Uncomfortable as they sometimes were, those few small lessons were worth gold to me and moved me sufficiently forward to win a three-year writing grant shortly after finishing his course.

Then I dropped out of college for the second time and took a few independent workshops, but I never stayed for long — my experience of them was of a bunch of people who didn't know what they were doing running off at the mouth under the weak leadership of slightly accomplished writers. Rightly or wrongly, I felt they were offering bad advice that would only confuse my search. Still, I didn't believe in myself and I didn't know what to do; the only thing I knew was that I *had* to write — in any event I kept coming back to it.

I wish that someone at that time had told me to read Rainer Maria Rilke's *Letters to a Young Poet*, a book I urge all of my students to read now. In it, he says things like:

"There is no measuring with time, no year matters, and ten years are nothing. Being an artist means not reckoning and counting, but ripening like the tree which does not force its sap and stands confident in the storms of spring without the fear that after them may come no summer. It does come. But it comes only to the patient, who are there as though eternity lay before them... I learn it daily, learn it with pain to which I am grateful: *patience is everything!*"

And quoting his own mentor, Rodin: "It is necessary always to work."

And, "Prose needs to be built like a cathedral: there one is truly without a name, without ambition, without help: on scaffoldings, alone with one's consciousness."

And, "Works of art are of an infinite loneliness," and "in one creative tought a thousand forgotten nights of love revive," and "...go into yourself and test the deeps in which your life takes rise; at its source you will find the answer to the question whether you *must* create."

If you feel that you could live without writing, he said, then you must not attempt it at all. But even to discover that is a great discovery.

I once taught in a workshop where I tried to convey that message, and the program director called me aside to ask that I refrain from discouraging the students. To attend a workshop that fears and attempts to sidestep that solitary query is a waste of time.

"Why," Rilke asked, "do you want to shut out of your life any agitation, any pain, any melancholy, since you really do not know what these states are working upon you."

You can buy that Rilke book from W. W. Norton in a splendid translation by M.D. Herter Norton for $6.95, and it is worth a thousand dollars worth of workshops — more, far more.

I wish I had had it when I was twenty-five. I did, however, have the good advice of Alexander Blackburn, then editor of *Writer's Forum* in Colorado; he said simply, in an open letter to young writers, "If you can quit, probably you should." Valuable advice to me in my twenties because it helped me recognize I could not quit.

You may ask what help that is if one cannot quit anyway, but recognizing the fact that one cannot quit and going on is not the same as expending spirit on a vain wish to quit that which has irrevocably chosen you. In his epic lament on the death of Dylan Thomas, Kenneth Rexroth bemoans the manner in which the poetic instinct in our society is quashed rather than nourished: "How many, on the advice of their analysts, decided a business career would be best after all?"

Sometimes I believe the answer to that question is none. For a poet cannot make that choice; if a poet needs the money, he or she will find room for both — like T. S. Eliot, Wallace Stevens, so many others. And no workshop of any seriousness has any business discouraging its participants from considering the ultimate question: Am I really a writer? Must I write?

Akin to Rexroth's question, though more illuminating I think, is a statement by Saul Bellow: "The old philosophy distinguished between knowledge achieved by effort (*ratio*) and knowledge received (*intellectus*) by the listening soul that can hear the essence of things and comes to understand the marvellous. But this calls for unusual strength of soul. The more so since society claims more and more and more of your inner self and infects you with its restlessness. It trains you in distraction, colonizes consciousness as fast as consciousness advances. The true poise, that of contemplation or imagination, sits right on the border of sleep and dreaming."

But I am not here to knock the *ratio* of workshops. I am here to sort through what I know of them and share my knowledge of them, such as it is. And to say that attending an MFA program, when I was ready for it, made all the difference for me as a writer. As an MFA student, I had the opportunity to work and talk with great and dedicated teachers like Gordon Weaver, Gladys Swan, Andre Dubus, W. D. Wetherell, Jack Myers, and to spend hours upon hours discussing craft and art with fellow seekers. The work in the classroom and workshop sessions and the lectures were important, but the talk that went on afterwards, often into the wee hours of what might otherwise have been a dark night of the soul, was equally so. And I began to find my way, began to find the place I sought and, finally, to achieve that most advantageous place of learning about writing — the place of the writing teacher.

I have taught various forms of workshop from the one-time one-hour session to sessions lasting from a weekend to a month, sessions where the participants live together for a fortnight, immersing themselves in the writing life all the waking hours of the day and night and sessions where people come to class for a few hours and go home until the next day. I've taught by writing exercises, one-on-one conferences, group-run as opposed to leader-directed workshops, in junior college, undergraduate, and master's and PhD degree writing programs, by delivering a series of craft lectures, and in programs independent of any university, attended sometimes by people who have already achieved a considerable level of artistic accomplishment — some who have already published one or more books, but who have run aground and need a shoulder to help nudge them back to the water. I have team-taught with brilliant colleagues — Robie Macauley, Gordon Weaver, Alexandra Marshall, Pamela Painter, James Carroll, Askold Melnyczuk, Alexandra Johnson — and I have had the benefit of brilliant students in my workshops.

What is best?

A lot depends on how much time you have, how much money, how long and successfully you have been writing.

How much time and money you have only you can answer. The question of how successfully you have been writing is more difficult, though not impossible to answer. If you are working with serious commitment, intensely, devoting a reasonable amount of time at least a couple or more times a week to a deep and intense reading of good writing and a deep and intense attempt to ignite the source of language within you, you will find yourself approaching the place where your stories are. And I believe that when you feel yourself near that place is when you will begin to profit most from guidance.

It is rather like hunting for amber on the beach. Sometimes you find pretty little yellow pebbles that you want very much to believe are amber, even though in your heart you know they are not amber, but mere glittery bits of dead stone. But the value of those pretty little yellow stones is that you do learn to know them, to know that they are *not* amber, to *know* that which is not amber. And then suddenly, as if by chance, you find a *real* piece of amber, and you have no doubt. You can tell by the way the light strikes and illuminates it, by its elegant lightness in your palm, by its irregular shape and texture (as opposed to the dull smoothness of stone), by the feel of it against your fingertips, by the sound it makes when you tap it against your tooth — not hard and sharp like stone, but the quiet sound of a thing that was once alive, a thing that gives a bit, and when you peer into it, you see its mysterious glow, sometimes even the spectre of ancient fossils trapped within — a chip of ancient history, or even a fistful of it.

My first three published stories, which came after many pieces of worthless dross (worthless except that I learned a little something from each of them, when I was able to suspend my fear of failure sufficiently to receive the lesson), were like those pretty little yellow pebbles. The fourth one was amber, and I had no doubt — I knew as I wrote it that it was coming from the place in me I had searched so long for, the place where the stories I could write were, the stories that it seems I was meant to write. You know when you are there.

The first time you find and truly begin to know that place, I believe, is when you really are ready to benefit from a good workshop or tutorial. Workshops and courses and lessons and books on craft and the study of the masters can help lead you to that moment if you are willing to suspend your fear and self-doubt sufficiently to learn the lessons you can only learn from your failed stories, from stooping on the beach to pick up those pebbles which are *not* the real thing but which — by scrutinizing them — help prepare you, by a process of elimination, to identify what *is* the real thing when you find it, that recognizing a flaw in what you are writing is not a failure, but a success, occasion for joy.

What I am getting at here in more concrete terms, I think — though it is difficult to be concrete about a process as slipperily alive and multifaceted as writing — is what I attempt to teach in my workshops and what the most alert workshop participants are seeking to learn. We walk around and around and around it, this thing that is at once so enormous and so infinitesimally minute we fail to see it, or which is so brilliant we cannot look head on at it, or which is so cunningly and richly ordinary we walk right past it.

My aim as a workshop leader is not to help a participant to successfully complete a given piece of writing, but to help her or him find the way into the process. To publish one story, encouraging and pleasant as that may be, is not the key; the key is to find the place in you where the stories are that you can write, want to write, even *need* to write. The thing is not merely to get there and bring back a single story, not to find a single piece of glowing amber, but to learn to recognize the glow, to study the route to the place of the stories so that you can find your way back there again, even if the walls of the tunnel have caved in behind you on your way out.

It is learning to accept and grasp the imagination as a faculty while at the same time developing your craft so that the skills become second nature and are instantly available to be placed at the disposal of your imagination when it sends for them. Your craft is the tools you need to shore up the tunnel as it caves in, so you can go on.

Thus the question of what sort of workshop or writing course you take is probably less important than your own readiness judiciously to receive that which helps you find the inner path to your own source, judiciously to reject that which does not, and intensely to focus on the lessons of craft available from all the great masters who have come before us.

So: You want to study writing. What should you do? Write. Read the masters. Read the poets. Be patient; time is nothing. Study. Listen. Allow yourself to fail and to learn the lessons your own failure affords you. Listen to the advice of your peers and of your teachers, but listen judiciously, select that which might be of use, humbly reject that which is not. Attend courses, workshops, lectures, readings. Talk, intoxicate yourself on talk about the craft and the art. As Jack Kerouac suggested, Write long wild letters about it all, read long wild letters about it with an open heart.

Ask yourself if you really *must* write, and if the answer is yes, receive that blessing and recognize that you have chosen yourself for the study of a lifetime.

A HARMONY OF SECRETS: TALKING TO MYSELF

Q: Where shall we start?
A: In the middle of things.

Q: Something I always wondered, when is the best time to write?
A: When you're supposed to be doing something else. The muse loves a desperado.

Q: Do you believe in the muse, then? In some manner of super- or subliminal inspiration?
A: Yes.

Q: Which is it? Super or sub?
A: If I knew the answer to that it could be neither I think. However, I do know that stories sometimes come to me as if whispered into my ear by some being. Those, I think, are perhaps the best of them if I am at all entitled to make such a statement about my own work. Other stories, however, are constructed in fits of more or less conscious inspiration. Still others rise spontaneously in a kind of semi-conscious inspiration brought on by great agitation — as when I did a job for Copenhagen's Torture Rehabilitation Center editing their psychiatric manual for therapists working with torture survivors; the material was so disturbing that I was compelled to write two stories when I was done, incorporating bits and pieces of the material which had eaten into my mind in order to assure myself that there was a good counterbalancing this evil, this ugliness.

Q: Do you understand your own fiction?

A: I usually do eventually come to understand my stories, but not for a while. Sometimes I get them right off, even as I am writing them sometimes I can see the "meaning" of it, but rarely. That is with what seem to me weaker pieces — stories which are illustrations of thoughts, where everything fits in like a piece of an equation, and equations of course are a kind of tautology: 2 apples plus 3 apples minus 1 apple equals 4 apples. A man and a woman waiting for a train to take them for an abortion discuss the decision, and the countryside on one side of the track is fertile, on the other side barren. One decision equals this, the other equals that; his wish equals aridity, hers fertility. It's good, but it's so comprehensible, so accessible. Where is the mystery? The cryptic stuff of life?

Which is not the same as saying the story has no meaning. Hopefully, its "meaning" is complex enough to embody, fictionally, some large aspect of existence, to encompass and convey some sense of recognition and wonder, some visitation of the sublime or divine which, as Shelly suggested, the words of poetry (or fiction) redeem from decay.

However, thinking about one of my stories that seemed overly clear to me, which made me fear it was simplistic, I have found that some people who read it, gifted readers, do not "get" it, so...

Miguel de Unamuno says, "The reader looking for a finished novel does not deserve to be my reader; he is already finished himself before he begins reading me." That is part of this same danger. Being finished before you even start. Carolyn Kizer: "I think it's very dangerous to start with a purpose in mind. I also think it's pretty dangerous to construct a poem from ideas. Poems are made of little disparate snapshots — little bits of imagery — and then suddenly a big image will come along and magnetize all those little scraps... They come together and then *that's* what makes the poem. Ideas have very little to do with it." For poem I think we can substitute story.

26

Q: Alice McDermott says that the writer must, after writing a story, become a "calm reader" who "must ultimately make sure that in the overwhelming rush (of inspiration) inspired words are correctly chosen and fully meaningful and that the piece of fiction works as a whole." She quotes Borges who called reading "an action subsequent to writing and more resigned, more civil, more intellectual."

A: I like that — that reading is more intellectual than writing. And I would certainly agree with Ms. McDermott and of course with Borges and with Wordsworth, too, who spoke of the act of writing as "the spontaneous overflow of emotion...recollected in tranquility." Only one phrase in Ms. Mc Dermott's statement would I wish to advise caution with: "fully meaningful." You can kill a living thing with an overdose of meaning. I like what Archibald MacLeish said about this in his *Ars Poetica*. "A poem should not mean, but be." Meaning is more the realm of the critic than the writer. The critic pinches and pokes the text to make it produce a circumscribable significance, but the writer's task is, to my mind, best defined by William Blake: "I will not reason and compare, my business is to create..."

Sometimes, often, it is necessary for the reader not merely to exercise what Poe called the "kindred art" of reading, but actually to invent the "meaning" of a poem or story, maybe it is always necessary for the reader to invent the meaning of any text. But the text has to be good enough to facilitate that invention.

And again, I am not saying that this is the *only* way. But where there is complexity there is multiplicity of meaning. And in the end, perhaps it is a question of what control the writer has over his or her material. E. M. Forster said that his characters would often take over the fiction on him, to which Nabokov replied that he could understand the characters mutinying on that tedious voyage to India, but his own characters were gally slaves.

Sometimes it is difficult to know if the detail one selects is arbitrary and whether that matters. I would be hard-pressed to explain every detail in every story I write, but I am reluctant to start monkeying with something that *feels* right — that's a good way to make something that happened to unhappen. It troubles me sometimes when my creative decisions seem cloudy, but that can also be a kind of hubris, a kind of arrogance; I wish to be greater than the process. I want to call the shots here. I'm the boss. That's a good way to talk yourself into a writer's block.

Calvino said something very interesting about this: "Poetry is the great enemy of chance in spite of also being a daughter of chance and knowing that, in the last resort, chance will win the battle. One throw of the dice will never annul chance."

I — my conscious self — am part of the process, but I am by far not all of the process. What I come up with often is offered up from murky sources; other times, I stumble upon something in the world that I recognize as valuable "material". Mary Sharrat tells me how on the island of Hiva Ua in French Polynesia where Gaugin and Jacques Brel went to die, she was bitten on the leg by a centipede and was ill for a week, nearly dying. Instantly I can see that this would make a powerful bit in a fiction (though I won't steal it from her — she is a writer herself); that is something in the world, informed by history, facts, etc., all of which are charged with connotative significance. Other fictional bits however simply flow out of the murk within or are roiled up by others.

Two friends at lunch once turned to me and said, "We have been talking about you and we have decided you should kill your angel." I had no idea what they meant, but the statement instantly produced an image in my mind of an angel in a basement, cowering, its life threatened. From that image, produced by that unexplained statement, came a story which was important to me and which may never have been written without that stimulus. But where did it come from?

Q: Do you ever write according to a scheme, plan the fiction out first?
A: Never. I know some people do, but I have a feeling that's often plot fiction — often, but not always, non-literary fiction. I

do often have a period with a story and always with novels where I am having spurts of inspiration, bits of scenes, scraps of dialogue, disconnected detail, that I will jot down and keep close to hand for when I am actually writing the story, glancing from the pad from time to time to see where and if those jotted notes fit in. Sometimes I can glimpse far ahead in what I'm writing. But if I try to plan it all out first, it dies on me, it loses its passion, spontaneity, life. Who was it said, No surprise for the writer, no surprise for the reader? A good fiction has a span greater than that of the human consciousness — at least greater than *this* human's consciousness. It comes from someplace deeper than the surface. It's like Wright Morris said, "How do I know what I want to say until I've said it?" He also said, "Change your syntax and you change your mind." Flannery O'Connor said, "I write to discover what I know," and William Faulkner called his fiction process "lying my way to the truth." However, there is a difference, of course, between plain lying and trying to make psychological, spiritual, existential sense of experience.

I don't know what I think about something, good bad or indifferent, until i start to explain it to myself in words, and in the process of explaining it, of creating it, fleshing it out so I can *see* it — whether rhetorically or fictionally or whatever — I eventually discover what I "mean," even if that discovery is only a long, contemplative walk around the ineffable. It seems to me thought runs much deeper than the conscious mind — it has to be invited up on the flow of words. And where do the words come from? Really? Again, they are handed up from somewhere, but where? "Who hath put wisdom in the inward parts? Or who hath given understanding to the heart?" That from Job (38:36) and it is the Lord speaking (albeit through His author).

Gladys Swan once told me that her stories seemed to come through her on their way to some unknown destination. It is a great and wondrous mystery. I do recognize that I build my stories out of flecks of my own hair and nails and spit, but that is just the visible stuff, the stuff that sticks to the spirit of the story like talcum on an air current or the violin that gives sound to the graph of notes. What the story actually is seems to me something quite else. A good story to my mind is not a moral lesson or an ideological tract or a sociological study, but a glimpse of the mystery of life unfolding. Of course, it can be all of those things, both and, but the literary hit I am after is one that *only* fiction or poetry can give, not one that could be done by one of the social sciences as well. That's just a matter of taste of course.

Q: You spoke before about "plot" fiction and "non-literary" fiction. What is the difference between literary and non-literary fiction.

A: Reading a book of non-literary fiction is a bit like going to a B movie on a sunny afternoon. You go and sit in the dark for a while looking up at these big bright images on the screen and your entire life is on hold out beyond the circle of darkness. Then the film is over and you stumble out into the daylight which is so sharp your head and your eyes ache, and you are reminded of all the problems you were slipping away from when you bought the ticket for the flick that you could hardly afford in the first place. Reading a book of literary fiction (or seeing a great film — like the one made from Knut Hamsun's *Hunger* or Joyce's *Ulysses* or Fellini's *La Strada* or most any Bergman and a couple of Van Trier's and Winterberg's *Celebration* and Jarmulsch's *Dead Man* or Pasolini's *Oedipus Rex* to name but a few) takes you away from that troublesome quotidian reality for a while, too, but when it delivers you back to your life, you are changed — you see things a bit differently, your view of the reality that is existence, your comprehension of your own limitations is sharper. Perhaps you are a little sadder, but you are also a little bit less frightened — or you are frightened in a constructive sense, in the way that classic tragedy produces pity and fear, exposes and saves you from your own hubris. You are not less alone, but you have a greater understanding of the fact that we are all essentially alone, and perhaps a greater determination to try to make contact with another of the fellow islands peopling your universe, one of whom in fact has just made profound contact with you, has opened his or her soul to evoke an opening of your own, the mutual process revealing a harmony of secrets.

Q. You used the term "plot fiction" with what seemed a note of disdain.

A: I just don't ever think about plot. To my way of thinking a story has to grow the way a plant or a tree does, naturally, organically. Of course, as Calvino says, "Just as in poems and songs, the rhymes help to create the rhythm, so in prose narrative there are events that rhyme." But just as I would not consult a rhyming dictionary to try to fill in a rhyme that does not come up on my breath, neither would I begin to draw an Aristotelian diagram to be certain the upward slope of my plot moves evenly toward climax or drops sharply enough toward denouement. Others might find this useful, but it is not my way. Plot and character grow from seeds too deep in the loam of my unconscious for me to worry them. However, I do use the dictionary a lot.

Q: What about happy endings?
A: Lies.

Q: Well, upbeat endings then?
A: More lies.

Q: Is life really so miserable?
A: Life is glorious. But each life ends in death, and death may be many things from tragic to profound, timely, untimely, haunting, heart-rending, brutal, sad, even welcome, but I do not think it possible to adequately describe an event as inevitable, complex and full of dread as death with the word happy. Likewise I think that serious literature deals with the complexity of our life, with the insufficiency of our intellectual equipment to encompass the fact

31

that we come out of the dark to live for a time in the light before returning to the dark again, and we know not how or why; during our prolonged moment in the light we find partners with whom we couple and produce new players to remain behind when we have shuffled off. And, as Octavio Paz says, "When we dream and when we couple we embrace phantoms," or Borges, "Waking is another dream that dreams of not dreaming and...the death we fear in our bones is the death that every night we call a dream." Our lives with these phantom partners and other fellow players, all of whose inner lives are invisible to us, made visible only obliquely by their report, run their own complex courses, all of which is further complicated by the fact that we have to eat, to consume, ingest other life in order for our own lives to keep ticking. Fairly brutal conditions even if we have assigned all the killing to food factory workers and keep it far from sight where millions of miserable chickens and cows and pigs are forced to live under evil conditions. Unless we are addicted to *Animal Planet*, we rarely have to see a tiger with blood-smeared maw, and having made such arrangements, perhaps we would prefer that William Blake revise "The Tyger" to give it a more upbeat ending and give him a cozy nickname — Tony, perhaps — so the reader can better "identify" and "empathize" with him.

Our bodies need nourishing food to remain healthy and survive, and our minds and souls need spiritual and psychological nourishment as well. We can no sooner survive on a diet of popcorn than our spirits and intellects can continue soundly on nothing but *Spin City*, *David Letterman*, *Jay Leno*, and John Grisham. Happy or upbeat endings are devices dreamed up by publishers who want to slip their hands into the pockets of the sleeping masses without waking them from their uneasy slumber of false contentment.

Ibsen says it in his final play from 1899 — a review of which was Joyce's first publication, at the age of seventeen — *When We Dead Awaken*:

We only see what we have missed

When we dead awaken.

And what then do we see?

We see that we have never lived.

Our entertainment industry goes to great pains not to wake the dead.

Into the same category I would place all the inspirational horseshit that sells so well. *Chickensoup for the Geekbrain*... Okay, there is room for everything from simple entertainment to profound art, and dedication to causes and sociological tracts can also be useful, but we live in a society obsessed by popcorn: there's sports popcorn, actionfilm popcorn, computergame popcorn; TV sitcom and soap popcorn, talkshow popcorn, and so-called "literary" popcorn.

The entertainment media seems convinced that the vast majority of the population would apparently rather watch and hear about Tiger Wood's latest triumph for a couple of hours than see a production of *Hamlet* or *Macbeth* or read an equivalent novel, whether classic or contemporary, or god forbid, some stories or poems. But what, I wonder, do you have simmering in your brain to console yourself against the dark when you lay down to sleep after an evening with Tiger Wood? A slow motion replay of him whacking a long drive on repeat?

Q: Isn't one of the problems that contemporary fiction and poetry has become too obsessed with "experiment" for experiment's sake? Can ordinary mortals hope to understand all this egghead stuff without an advance degree in literature?

A: A successful experiment is an innovation and leads to a new way of expressing and perceiving something of our existence. A novel like James Joyce's *Ulysses*, for example, which is probably more discussed than read, is an innovatively complex fictional presentation of western culture which functions on many levels. If one takes Homer as the beginning, so to speak, of western cultural history, embodying classical Greek values and symbols upon which our culture builds, then Joyce's novel might be seen in many ways as the conclusion or counterbalance, two plus millennia later. Joyce's *Ulysses* parallels the journey of Homer's Ulysses from the Trojan War back to Ithaca where his wife Penelope, holding off many suitors who think Ulysses dead, and their son Telemachus, await his return, with the story of a single day in 1904 in the life of a Dublin Jew, Leopold Bloom, who spends the day of June 16th walking around Dublin in the knowledge that his wife is at home committing adultery with a man named Blazes Boylan. The chapters of Joyce's *Ulysses* roughly parallel the episodes of Homer's epic, and the levels of meaning of the book are myriad. One of its aims is to celebrate the human body, so each chapter is also characterized by a body organ — for example, in one chapter, Leopold Bloom defecates while a church bell rings in the background, a brilliant literary response to the church's hypocritical suppression of human bodily joy. The fact that Bloom is a pacifist everyman, a non-macho, non-nationalist humanist, as an emblem of modern 20th century society, contrasts with Homer's representation of Ulysses, a heroic warrior journeying home to his faithful wife, and makes a profound and prophetic observation of our times - feminist, pacifist, anti-jingoist, contra-dogmatist, etc. Among the many other things that Joyce's novel does is to parody, chapter for chapter, various writing genres, styles and techniques, and also introduces and develops William James's concept of the stream of consciousness, via an interior monologue technique also employed and developed by others, perhaps most notably Virginia Woolf.

While I can only agree that some of the other "experiments" in the book may fairly be viewed as boring and as largely inaccessible to anyone without critical guidance as to what Joyce is doing, the interior monologues — most particularly those of Leopold and of Molly Bloom — changed the face of the twentieth century even, I would venture, for those who have never read Joyce. I base this on my own experience with the book. When, at the age of 24, I read the Bloom soliloquies for the first time, then heard them interpreted on record by E. G. Marshall and Siobhan

Mackenna, I was instantly changed, brought into a profoundly more intimate contact with my own consciousness, recognized at once the possibility of accessing one's own deeper thought processes and the simultaneity of time as a feature of our psychological make-up.

Today, nearly eighty years after *Ulysses* first publication, stream of consciousness is no longer considered avant garde; it is a standard feature of our literary lives throughout the world.

This is the kind of power that literary experiment can have. So even if some experimental fiction is a challenge to read and some readers may not wish to accept that challenge, it is nonetheless an important feature of our literature, of our culture, of our lives as human beings (as opposed, say, to our lives as zombies).

In any event, I do not think that many sensitive readers — whether or not they are English majors — would fail to be moved by the Bloom soliloquies, most notably Molly's gorgeous celebration and affirmation of human life and sexuality on which the last hundred pages or so of the book flows, concluding with her resounding *Yes*.

Probably many, perhaps most people are afraid of Joyce, would have a block against even cracking the cover of *Ulysses*. Perhaps the problem is that our educational systems are not sufficiently vigorous in teaching people to be active readers. Borges identifies "good readers (as being)... as singular, and as awesome, as great authors themselves."

A reader ideally recapitulates the work of the writer, performs a "kindred art," follows the map of the text across the same terrain and perhaps sees what the author has described, perhaps other things as well, perhaps different things.

I have had readers whose comments have inspired me to new insights on my own fiction. I also had a somewhat naive, though delightful, question about a story which, in my attempt to answer it, inspired me to write a sequel to the story which was its own, I think, valid statement.

So to get back to the question, no, I do not think that contemporary fiction is obsessed with experiment for experiment's sake. In fact, most fiction being published today is not at all experimental. A very great deal of it, I would venture to say, is doing the same old thing in the same old way, and that's how many commercial publishers want it; they don't want to wake the sleeping reader, they don't want him to want something new or other because then they will have to revise their program and risk losing money.

We saw a brief great flourishing of interest in innovative fiction in the Sixties and Seventies with writers like Italo Calvino, Samuel Beckett, Borges, Marquez, Robert Coover, Donald Barthelme, John Barth, John Hawkes, William H. Gass, and others. For those few years, words like metafiction, self-reflexive fiction, surrealism, fabulism, etc., were not, as they are for the most part today in the wake of the "dirty-realist" steamroller, unwelcome. "Postmodernists need not apply."

It is interesting that the man who coined, or perhaps purloined, that phrase "dirty-realism" as a catchy tag for a *Granta* anthology in the 1980s, followed up by a next issue tagged "More Dirt" and prefaced by a statement on fiction that was indeed pure manure, is now fiction editor of *The New Yorker* — perhaps one should call it *The New New Yorker*, although I am not convinced he is interested in any manner of newism or neo-newism.

Any number of contemporary literary journals and small presses, however, provide a greatly needed forum for fictional innovation and otherness where virtually all the genres can live together in exciting peace and where the truth of Wallace Stevens' statement — "The vegetation abounds with forms." — is recognized.

Generally speaking, I think people who insist that all fiction must be "realistic" have problems seeing the difference between life and art. I have a framed print on my wall of René Magritte's realistic painting of a pipe which he captions, *"Ceci n'est pas une pipe."* ("This is not a pipe.") It hangs among some very strange non-realistic other-worldly originals I have by the Italian artist Giancarlo Savino. Not abstract, but very strange, faces from another dimension peering out from the canvas. I love nothing better than to have someone focus on the Magritte and says, "This is not a pipe. Then what the hell *is* it?"

The answer, obviously, is, "A picture of a pipe." Which some people find *very* pedantic — those are the ones I'm after, for it is to them, to that attitude in *us*, that Magritte addresses his painting. The pigments in the painting could as well have been used to form any number of other images — a tree, a boat, an abstract...

Funnily enough, most people today would not dream of hanging on their wall a painting whose subject was clearly identifiable for that is no longer the central realm of painting, but of photography; however, when it comes to fiction, they want — to quote the late great Raymond Carver — "the real things that really matter to real people."

Hey, John Cheever is one of my greatest literary heroes — Chekhov and Dubus, too, but they're not the only game in town, and to quote Cheever, "Literature is not a competitive sport," god rest his enormous soul, even if Norman Mailer reports that when he reads a book he does so in cool competition, comparing the author's skills and strengths and weaknesses with his own, as a boxer or football player might.

Q: Following your logic, I wonder, do your characters look like human beings?
A: Let me respond with a question of my own. What is this:

- -

1

-

Q: A man's face?
A: Ha! Gotcha! *Ceci n'est pas une visage d'un homme.*

37

Q: Okay, pedant, a representation of a face?

A: No, it is an arrangement of three short lines and one slightly longer one that possibly suggest a human face. Just as the sentence "A man walked down the street" is only six words, but creates the setting of a whole scene limited only by the reader's imagination. I guess what I am trying to say here is that only my readers know what my characters look like, and I suppose they look different to each reader. My sister amazed me once by calling me up to tell me that there was a woman on television who had the same voice as the voice of one of the women in my novel *The Book of Angels*. I was flabbergasted that she could "hear" the voices of characters in a fiction in that sense. I tend to hear a character's voice speaking dialogue, but not as specifically as that unless I am taking the character or the dialogue from life (for example, the woman taxi driver in the story "Kansas City" was a real taxi driver I once rode with at four in the morning and who told me the strange things that the driver in that story tells the main character in that story, Johnny Fry — whose name, by the way, is the name of the first Pony Express rider, which seemed appropriate to my Johnny Fry's mission in life.)

But I rarely describe a character unless some physical trait is relevant. In "The Great Master," for example, the character who decides to consume all the food in his house grows fatter and fatter. So obviously, the reader would be seeing a very fat man in that story. Also there is one character in it who is blind in one eye, and the blind eye is milky blue, another has a shaven head and wears saffron robes and red running shoes, but the scene in which they appear needed these physical details for grounding.

When a story is told through one character's point of view, the physical appearance of other characters will appear through his or her eyes, but still, usually only minimally. In "Dust," for example, the psychiatrist named Dr. Saltine is an Adlerian (Adler was a very small man who developed the theory of the inferiority complex) and his feet don't quite reach the floor when he sits down. And another character — a magician — is described from a photograph I saw of Aleister Crowley, a kind of in-joke for those who know.

But my characters are shades of human beings whether described as such or not, and I suppose it is fair to presume that they possess all the equipment of all human beings, unless otherwise specified. Oh, I have also written about characters who are a voice without a body, a character who is only feet, etc., in the metafiction titled "Noses in Fiction" (included elsewhere in this book) which is inter alia a metaphor for the relationship between god and man, great fun, but no matter what you do in fiction — even in my stories told through the point of view of snails, flies, ants, wasps — unless you go completely abstract, which is hard to imagine, it tends to fit the homocentric view, just as in most abstract paintings, viewers tend to discern representational forms.

As a writer, what I see of my characters is only more or less abstract suggestions that glimmer vaguely on the fuel of language, breath and words, referring to more or less generic "images" — man, woman, house, child. Occasionally an evoked detail creates a sense of solidity — a jagged scar, a green eye — but such details exist as occasional evocations on an abstract canvas, anchoring spots to aid the uncertain psyche, to keep it from missing the conjured sphere. Basically, I think what I "see" of characters in other people's fiction that I read is similar to what I see of my own — much like the faces in a dream; generally in mist, occasionally swooping right up into your own face.

I had a teacher once who told me he had published a novel which included an annex giving supplemental details about the "lives" of all the characters: parents' names, where they went to school, how much they earned, etc., as if they had lives at all!

It is important to remember that words are magical. Remember how people used to, maybe still do, substitute make-shift expletives to avoid pronouncing certain very powerful words — "gosh" for "God," "gee" for "Jesus," "down there" for "cunt." When Norman Mailer published *The Naked and the Dead* and James Jones *From Here to Eternity*, it was still illegal to publish the word "fuck" so they salted their soldiers' dialogue with "fug" and "frig" to avoid that issue. Everyone knew what it meant, but somehow concealing the word behind an expletive mask quelled its power to alarm or offend. Ironically, such exercises further preserve the primitive aura of such words. Today, with songs, television, radio, print filled with four-letter words, the power is greatly depleted.

I attended an amusing luncheon at an academic conference not long ago at which a Finnish delegate opened the conversation by asking in a sincere manner with an ingenuous smile, speaking slowly with very precise enunciation as Finns are wont to do, "Something I do not understand about the English language. Can a woman be an ass-hole?"

Some of the people at the lunch — particularly one blond woman lawyer from Chicago — were from a pretty conservative organization, and the Finnish question caused a bit of uncertainty until he explained sincerely that he only wanted to know if that word, as an insult, could be applied to man and woman alike. Someone offered that "bitch" would more likely be the word of choice for a woman, whereas another thought "bitch" was rather the feminine counterpart of "bastard."

"You can also call a man a prick," someone else offered, whereupon the eyes of the blond Chicago lawyer narrowed, and she said sternly, "But there is one word I would advise you *not* to apply to a woman in the United States, at least not in Chicago."

I could not resist saying, "What? Cunt?" And her sharp eyes turned toward me. After an intense and — pardon me — pregnant moment in which she clearly was considering whether or not to thrash me, she mercifully relaxed and said, "You *dickhead*."

In a way, I am sorry I exposed the word to light as it seems to me about the last remaining magical word in the English language and is rapidly losing ground.

Still, all words are magic even if, as Aristotle suggested, "The word dog does not bite."

Q: You mention having named one charcter in a historical context. How do you generally name your characters?

A: I have a horror of naming a character something like Jim Clark, the name of some 1950s B film hero — I guess for fear it will get me thinking like those films, with tedious linearity.

In fact, the world is full of striking, evocative names. The main player of my first novel, *Crossing Borders* (Watermark Press, 1990), was Jack Sugrue, the name of a guy I knew as a kid. I borrowed his name because its mix of sounds and suggestions was perfect for my character, sweetness and rue, the surname of an Irish king with the given name of an everyman.

The right name can bring the character and the fiction to life. In my novel *The Book of Angels* (Wordcraft of Oregon, 1997), I named the main character Michael Lynch simply because I liked the name. Afterwards, however, I realized that "Michael" was the name of a warrior angel, and the name Lynch kind of suggested "linchpin", something essential and strong. These traits were quite relevant, but the choice was not conscious. Had it been so, I probably would have rejected it. I don't want to choose too consciously in these matters; I want the name to come to me rather than vice versa.

Other names which have arrived to help co-create characters: *Bluett* in my novel *Beneath the Neon Egg* (excerpted in *Agni* in 1999 and *Frank* in 2001); that name is sometimes spelled *Blewett*, but I did not like the visual suggestion of that — I was after the suggestion of the color for my character, which in fact became his nickname, "Blue," perhaps because the "soundtrack" of the novel, John Coltrane's magnificent *Love Supreme*, was recorded on the Bluenote label. *Broccoli* in "Broccoli is a Vegetable" (*Vignette*, Vol 1, Issue 1, Summer 1995) was a boy who would be teased unmercifully because of his name, which ultimately would determine his fate — a case of the name making the man. *Gasparini* in "Gasparini's Organ" (in *Unreal City*, Wordcraft of Oregon, 1996) is the real life name of a man who manufactured street organs in the last century, and it was while seeing and touching such an organ in a museum that the story began to appear on a flow of words starting, "My name is Vincente Gasparini. I was born in sin, died in shame. I gave to life my art." *Charles Feuk*, the name of a character in a recent story titled "South American Getaway" (*World Wide Writers 5*, 1999) appeared to me on a namesign at a conference I attended shortly before writing the story; Professor Feuk was a keynote speaker and that name, suggesting as it does a kind of effed up version of the 'f' word, hinted to me the story of this man whose vitality was drowning in his own success. *Binzer* is the name of someone I have known for years, but suddenly one day noticed the name, jotted it down, and it became the name of the main character in my next story, about a man residing in a kind of bin of spiritual strangulation, name and story seeming to come together in a kind of spontaneous combustion ("Cast Upon the Day," in *Arts & Letters*, Georgis State University, 1999).

The world is a goldmine of names, rich in variety and sound. The other day I saw the name "Bill Phantongphay" in a newspaper article, and I am itching to discover what story lies hidden in its stone. Not long ago I met a woman named Karen Golightly and was amazed to discover that Truman Capote had not invented that name. I am currently corresponding on an editorial project with a woman named "Layisha Laypang," and I know that name will become part of a fiction, even as the real-life Layisha remains a mystery to me, a person I never met and likely never will.

Q: From names to writer's block. Ever had one?
A: There is no such thing.

Q: Sorry?
A: Writer's block is a simple refusal to accept the words your imagination — or whatever faculty — hands up into your consciousness. Vincent Van Gogh gave the best advice I've ever heard about this in a letter to his brother Theo in 1884:

"Just slap anything on when you see a blank

canvas staring at you like some imbecile. You don't know how paralyzing that is, the stare of a blank canvas which says to the painter you can't do a thing. The canvas has an idiotic stare and mesmerizes some painters so much that they turn into idiots themselves. Many painters are afraid in front of the blank canvas, but the blank canvas is afraid of the real passionate painter who dares and who has broken the spell of 'you can't' once and for all."

Q: But what if you're not inspired?
A: If you're not inspired, just write. Don't doodle, *write*. Allow yourself to fail, but fail trying, not whimpering that you can't. And do not refuse to accept the words that come to you, do not turn them over again and again, sniffing them to determine whether they smell of shit, just write them as they come and let your pen fly on. If it wants to jump back and cross out, substitute another word, fine, let it, but keep moving and do not treat your muse with disrespect or suspicion. Remember what Henry Miller said: "If you don't listen when the muse sings, you get excommunicated." And he claims to have been horrified when she began to sing the tropics to him. "Oh, no, please, don't make me write *that*, they'll *kill* me!" You've got to listen, to write it down. She might only be clearing her throat, but get it down anyway.
    Heed Lu Ji's advice:
    "When instinct is swift as a horse, no tangle of
    thoughts will hold it back: a thought wind rises in
    your chest, a river of words pours out from your
    mouth..."
    And do not fear error. Remember what Van Gogh said:
    "If one wants to be active, one must not be afraid
    of going wrong...of making mistakes... Many
    people think that they will become good just by
    doing no harm — but that's a lie... That way lies

43

stagnation, mediocrity."

If you work hard and fast enough you may overwhelm your mental police or catch them sleeping so all the good stuff can break out of the locked door and fly through to your pen, your fingers.

Q: But what if you just can't?
A: Let yourself be driven by the terror of yet another day passing by without yielding anything of deep value — not necessarily something large, but just *something*. Even just a sentence, a paragraph, a moment's perception, the reading of a poem that widens the eyes with awe to remind yourself that awe exists in the realm of language, or allowing oneself to be wrapped for a moment in the skin of despair and master the terror of that by coolly observing how it feels in the tenderest part of the heart and writing that down, even just two sentences, and knowing that you have risen above, even for just a few moments, everything in life that wants to drag you down into the passive dust before your time has come.

Or try Franz Kafka's prescription:
"You don't have to leave your room.
Remain sitting at your table and listen.
Don't even listen, simply wait.
Don't even wait.
Be quite still and solitary.
The world will freely offer itself to you
To be unmasked. It has no choice.
It will roll in ecstasy at your feet.

Finally, don't allow yourself to be your own enemy. If there is a little man or a little woman sitting on your shoulder telling you that what you are writing is worthless shit, shrug the little creature off and go on, that's not the voice to listen to.

Q: What if you don't know *how*, don't know *what* to do?
A: Fake it. Hold your breath and jump. Lie. *Bullshit.* Pretty soon

you might find the lie is true and the bullshit is *good* bullshit.

Tear books from your shelves at random and feverishly read opening lines, last paragraphs, scraps of prose, priming yourself for an eruption of your own language.

Or look at it this way: You've suddenly found yourself in the cockpit of a plane and the pilot just died. Now *you're* the pilot. How the fuck did this happen?! That doesn't matter. You've got to fly the plane, you've got to land it. Radio for help! No — the radio's out, you're on your own. Oh, Christ, I *can't*!

Wait a second. Calm down. Either you're going to die or you're going to land this motherfucker. *Think*! What do you know about planes? A little bit of aerodynamics (theory), a little bit of stuff you've heard and glimpsed from other pilots. You use every goddamn thing you can. There is no morality up there, and you are not accountable for what you do, use everything you can beg, borrow, steal, break off, fold out. You've got to act and act fast and suddenly you're back to Van Gogh, that idiotic white sheet of paper trying to turn you into an idiot with its idiotic stare, but you have already decided: You *can*! You *will*! Or die trying.

So you grab hold of whatever is there — a scrap of voice, the glint in someone's eye at an inappropriate moment, the quality of light on the water glimpsed one morning out your front window, an inappropriate sentiment toward a loved one, the long shadow of a stranger on the street coming toward you, a turn of phrase, the music of a sentence in broken English, your boiling passion for the body of another human being, a little boy with a toy pistol, *whatever*, you grab it, and you *write*.

Q: Why do you write?
A: I write to complete the insufficiency of my understanding of my existence. I write fiction to try to complete that understanding as best I can, or at least to comment on it in a way that will soothe the wound which that incompleteness is.

In one of his private journals, John Cheever wrote, "I have been a storyteller since the beginning of my life, rearranging facts in order to make them more interesting and sometimes more significant." I like that.

One of the greatest statements I know on the process and motives of writing fiction is embodied in Sherwood Andersen's story "Death in the Woods," a very early and poorly understood example of metafiction, which is a story about the process of writing fiction as a metaphor for our creation of our own identities. Other splendid examples are John Barth's "Lost in the Funhouse," Robert Coover's "The Magic Poker" and "The Elevator," Francois Camoin's "Diehl: The Wandering Years" and Gordon Weaver's "The Parts of Speech," "The Interpreter," and "Ah Art! Oh Life!" In this volume I have also included one of my own, "Noses in Fiction."

Q: What is the single most important thing you have to say about writing fiction?
A: Go to the title essay of this book, "Realism & Other Illusions." Anything else.

Q: No. Thank you.
A: Thank *you*.

GETTING AROUND THE MIND:
HOW I READ, HOW I WRITE

My father used to read to us when we were kids, poetry mostly, and I loved it, loved hearing it, but never thought much about what it might *mean*. Perhaps what he read made the hair on my arms rise, made me stare out the kitchen window into the darkness and perceive mystery conjured by the music of the language and the images it produced.

Not until many years later, did I begin to think about stories *meaning* something, and I didn't much like the idea. By then I'd read a lot of Dostoevski and Camus and Gide and Sartre, Eliot, Joyce, Steinbeck, Huxley, Kerouac, Hemingway, and others, and these books bowled me over. Still, it never occurred to me that it should *mean* something. They were stories, fiction. M. Meursault drank café au lait at his mother's wake and had no ambitions and killed an Arab because the sun was blinding him and wound up in a jail cell grabbing a priest by his clerical collars and shouting, All your certainties are not worth one strand of hair from a woman's head! And then, awaiting his fate, he would run through all the possibilities of his undoing until finally he had come to the end of the list and found an hour's peace, and that anyhow was something.

To my eighteen year old mind, these were literal truths. They did not *mean* anything. They were not ideas. They were the facts of existence, experience, which I could view through the magical window of a book.

When Stephen Dedalus refused, on principle, to kneel and

pray at his mother's deathbed, this was simply something I might expect to happen to myself if I wasn't careful, and I wondered how I would respond to that literal event.

When Raskalnikov killed the old pawnbroker and the other woman, for me this did not happen in a novel in Russia in 1866; he did it in New York City, in the winter of 1961, when I read about it, and I wandered the freezing streets of Harlem in my version of a greatcoat, staggered at the thought of these acts we might be called upon to perform.

This is perhaps what John Fowles referred to in *The Magus* when his narrator talks about reading existential novels as prescriptions for behavior.

Then one day, it occurred to me that I had read a great many books and hadn't a clue what they *meant*. I don't exactly recall why or how I came to that conclusion. Perhaps it was a natural progression of maturation, a kind of molting of a pupal shell. Perhaps I met some bright person at C.C.N.Y. who talked literary circles around me. Whatever, I do remember that it was not fun.

Finally, I admitted to myself — after a struggle I was destined to lose — that I was ignorant. Utterly, abysmally ignorant. I understood nothing. I was a fake. I read and spouted, wrote essays in highschool, in college, and got good grades too, and I didn't understand a word of it. All I could do was feel. I could not think. I could persuade others, but I could not fool myself. Or if I knew anything at all, I did not know what that was.

Once I admitted that, though, I felt better. It was pleasant in a sense, smacking face first into this enormous wall of ignorance, and admitting it, saying, Yes, it is true, I am stupid, dumb, ignorant: I. Know. Nothing.

Only many years later would I read Wallace Stevens "Notes Toward a Supreme Fiction": "You must become an ignorant man again..." My ignorance was donned in ignorance, not as a literary exercise.

Then I had either to choose another field or do something about it. The only jobs available to me at that age if I dropped out of college were clerical ones. In fact, I spent a summer in an office on Wall Street when I was seventeen, another on Randall's Island two years later and without literature to console me, I might have perished there.

I had no hope but to try to figure it out. And that is kind of what I have been trying to do for the thirty-five years since, and still every time I approach a story or a poem — be it as a reader or as a writer — I get that feeling in my stomach I used to get when I was a schoolboy just before a fight it was too late to run or hide from or talk my way out of. Into the circle of leering faces and put up your dukes!

I started then, primed myself with books like John Ciardi's *How Does a Poem Mean?* and Mortimer J. Adler's *How To Read a Book*. Invariably hecklers on the subway who saw me slogging through those laudable texts could not resist asking me, "How *does* a poem mean?" or "How *do* you read a book?" as though the very questions were patently absurd.

I started by chance with a paperback I had bought shortly before the discovery of my ignorance, and I said to myself, "I am going to read this book, and I am going to understand it." The book, it so happened — by sheer luck — was John Barth's *The Floating Opera*. I say by sheer luck because that novel happens to be a work of metafiction — a fiction about the processes of fiction as a reflection of the process by which we create the fiction of our own identities and our own interpretations of reality. Metafiction is by no means new, but contemporary society in the sixties was ripe for it, for the hierarchical decay resulting from the death of God by then had found its way down to the grass roots and credible interpretations of objective reality were hard to come by.

I won't give a resumé of that novel, will suffice to say I put on my boxing gloves and went round and round with it, took notes, thought, meditated, referred, questioned, and by god, I began to *see*, I began to understand. I could *do* it!

Metaphors great and small detached themselves from the

action and undressed before my very eyes for my amusement and edification. Ironies stepped off the page to shake my hand and welcome me to the process and ask if I was having a good time.

Meaning stepped up and spoke its mind, and what it said was this: Existence is a state of partial blindness. (This was quantitatively different from what Pope had told me: "...to this due degree of heaven-bestowed blindness, submit!" No, this was a blindness to thrash about in and against.) Logic, I began to perceive, is vital to the building of bridges, to the practical application of aerodynamics, to the fabrication of an aspirin tablet, could tell me everything about the wasp (to paraphrase Dylan Thomas) except why. The realm of the rational intellect, I seemed to discern, is a practical one, and the blood that beats in our veins does not give two hoots about the philosophy of existentialism or any other for that matter.

We do not kill ourselves. This was one of the central themes of that Barth novel — a man trying to understand why he did not kill himself as his father had done. Because there is no earthly reason to do so, certainly no physical one, no biological one, no spiritual one, no emotional one — the only faculty suggesting to a healthy mind and spirit that one do so is a purely intellectual one.

Remember the character in Dostoevski's *The Possessed* who decides that existence is utterly without meaning, a state of enslavement to impending death; that we live beneath a boulder suspended on a rope above our heads waiting for the rope to snap, as it inevitably will. Under such circumstances, he reasoned, the only act of freedom is the freedom to decide when to cut the rope. And he decides to exercise this freedom. But an acquaintance, a political schemer, perceives that this could be useful; he proposes that our freedom-seeker not do the act until such time as it will be useful for the party cell — then he can sign a confession to some crime that another cell member had actually committed. Since life is meaningless and nothing matters, the man agrees, and in that agreement has reason to live a little longer. However, when the schemer comes to foreclose, the man discovers that things are not really so simple. All that his mind has instructed him to do is rebelled against by his body and he goes beserk. The mind, the intellect is not the only organ directing us.

This was, in fact, much the same as the conclusion of Barth's novel, and was closely aligned with the very sphere of doubt in which I found myself. What a coincidence that the book I should pick up at just the moment that I was determined to learn to understand should instruct me in this very truth I required. Perhaps not so surprising or coincidental, for the active reader with his kindred art does recapitulate the work of the author and co-creates its meaning. The fiction is a map of a land the reader recreates as he or she journeys through, and some of that countryside will be stamped with the character of the reader, just as what we see of the world is what our eye selects as being relevant to the circumstance of our soul.

We can, of course, turn to the critics for explanations to help us understand art. Often we *must* do so. Who in the world, for example, can read Joyce's *Ulysses*, say, without help? (And how ironic to read Richard Ellmann's interpretation of the French assessment of Joyce as lacking "the refined rationalism which would prove him incontestably a man of letters.") Aren't most of us warmly grateful, in general, for footnotes? And if we did not know that Camus was referring to Kierkegaard's *Leap of Faith* in *The Stranger,* we would miss some intellectual satisfaction, although we would not necessarily miss the impact and meaning of the story, the *experience* of it.

But what do we do when we are reading something so contemporary that little or nothing has been written about it yet? What if the writer is breaking some convention about which we are not even aware? What if the writer doesn't even care whether we understand? I have a Japanese friend who characterizes the difference between American and Japanese fiction with a movement of his hand: American fiction beckons — come in, come in! Japanese fiction raises a halting palm: keep your distance.

51

As with Joyce, Ellmann suggests, "There are no invitations, but the door is ajar."

Clearly, the more we read and more important, the more we read thoughtfully, the better equipped we will be to comprehend, but how exact *is* this science?

Now Mortimer J. Adler, in *How to Read a Book* says that reading is like playing catch. Either you catch the ball or you don't. Ezra Pound, too, in his remarkable *ABC of Reading* talks about the *science* of reading, but when he complained to Joyce that *Finnegans Wake* was unclear, Joyce said, *Well now Ezra, the action of the book takes place at night, is it not natural that what occurs in the dark will be unclear?*

John Ciardi was more helpful in *How Does a Poem Mean?* "The language of experience," he wrote, "is not the language of classification." And, "So for poetry, the concern is not to arrive at a definition and to close the book, but to arrive at an experience. There will never be a complete system for 'understanding' or for 'judging' poetry. Understanding and critical judgement are admirable goals, but neither can take place until the poem has been experienced, and even then there is always some part of every work of art that can never be fully explained and categorized." Which brings to mind John Barth's confession in one of his wonderful *Friday* essays that he is uneasy with students of literature because they do not seem to believe how important a part intuition plays in writing fiction.

In the mid to late eighties, as mentioned earlier, the great Raymond Carver talked about the fact that many writers of the sixties and seventies had gotten away from writing about the "real things that really matter to real people" — a statement that sought to dismiss all the previous decades of experiment in fiction, self-reflexive fiction, metafiction, etc. As Donald Barthelme once said, in what might have been a response, *Postmodernism is dead; I am hastening to tell all my postmodern friends to get out fast before their stock crashes.*

Carver was a wonderful writer, but realism is only one kind

of the great array of fictional forms. As Wallace Stevens said, The vegetation abounds with form. And as Gladys Swan says, "Vision dictates form." Form is something that grows with the fiction as a tree or a bush grows from the soil, slowly revealing its form.

I once bought a house in winter when its garden was bare; that spring, we watched the garden reveal itself, like a slow series of beautiful explosions — first the tiny white snowdrop buds, then the orange and purple aranthis popping up through the snow, then later the crocus, lillies, the tulips, the great yellow burst of forsythia, the magnolia... Of course it was all programmed in the earth — but perhaps our stories are, too. In go the seeds and the rain and the waste and the loss and the deaths and slowly the tale gathers itself to unfold — like Whitman's earth that "grows sweet things out of such corruptions."

How does the earth know that seed is a rose? What corruptions does it employ to tint the bloom so richly? What goes on down there in the black dirt?

Life does take place largely in the dark, and in the dark we must feel our way forward, *intuit,* must give ourselves over to the process of discovery. To me, intuition plays a great part in reading *and* writing, and sometimes I think the enemy is understanding. The fiction that can fit neatly into the brain seems to me a fiction of small proportions.

I spent a good few years trying to understand how much a writer ought to understand of his own story. I was crippled by my intellect, trying to create stories with meaning that could be netted like a butterfly, confined in a killing jar, pinned dead upon the page, ready for the part by part labelling. Indeed, some stories *can* be neatly explained, or need no explanation they are so transparent — some of Maupassant, most of O Henry, some Hemingway even (e.g. "Hills like White Elephants"), some Frank O'Connor stories with all their symbolism of political division.

Yet one of the most liberating moments for me as a writer was when I asked Robert Coover how much he feels he must comprehend of a story in progress and he said that perhaps the best of what he had written was that which he merely allowed to be written, where language took over and he became a mere tool of it. Gordon Weaver answered the question by saying, "Writing is a process of discovery."

Dylan Thomas described the process of his writing as "the rhythmic, inevitably narrative movement from an overclothed blindness to a naked vision," and Ezra Pound said, "Music begins to atrophy when it moves too far from the dance."

What do these things mean? What does a dance mean?

Writing, to me, *is* like a dance, though I am no dancer. It is my imagined dance. The dance of elements that comprise a story requires an existential agility, coordinating much more than the little core of consciousness that is our ego and our understanding. What does a tree mean? What does a bull mean?

My own approach can be summed up in the statement by Wallace Stevens in his powerful long poem, "Notes Toward a Supreme Fiction." Stevens called poetry the supreme fiction, but this can apply to both branches — remember F. Scott Fitzgerald's advice to young fiction writers: "Read the poets."

What Stevens advises is: not to impose, but to discover.

And, "Perhaps the truth depends on a walk around the lake" toward the "familiar music of the machine" setting up its balances — "not balances that we achieve, but balances that happen..." He also said in what I take as a metaphor for the act of writing: "The lion roars at the enraging desert/Reddens the sand with his red-colored noise," and "...the elephant/Breaches the darkness of Ceylon with blares..." There is that driving us to it, driving us to need to open up our voices — the enraging desert, the unbreached darkness. It happens in the chest, the lungs — Tadeusz Rózewicz's "struggle for breath," Pinsky's "column of air inside a human body."

Fiction, too, I think, at its best, is a physical act. For me the writing of fiction is something that must take place holistically, as an act of discovery which moves forward toward a delineation of the unknown, and it is no mere intellectual act. It forms on words in the heart, in the lungs, the throat, the syntax forged in the soul.

The poet Hölderin spoke of "the rhythm of representation" which his translator interpreted as "the pace at which verbal relations come to be perceived." In the writing of fiction, it is not only "verbal relations" but the relations of elements of forward movement in a story — the inevitable narrative of Dylan Thomas, the rhyming narrative events of Calvino.

John Updike compared the process of discovery in writing to driving at night — you can see no further than your headlights but if you keep driving, following those lights, you will get there — or somewhere.

How does that movement originate, generate? In character? Yes, I suppose it does. In "idea"? No doubt. In a preconceived event or series of events? Perhaps.

But to my mind, there is something even more basic than that. The *stuff* of which these elements are fashioned -- remember fiction is from *fictio*, to fashion, to shape. As Anthony Burgess put it: The sculptor fashions in stone, the painter in pigments, the writer in words.

Advice to a fiction writer from yet another poet, William Carlos Williams: "To write a short story is not to place adjectives, it is to learn to employ verbs in imitation of nature -- so that the pieces move naturally and watch, often breathlessly, what they *do*."

Dylan Thomas's *The force that through the green fuse drives the flower/Drives my green age; that blasts the roots of trees/Is my destroyer./And I am dumb to tell the crooked rose/My youth is bent by the same wintry fever...*

The action of our fiction is in our syntax, and syntax, Paul Valéry tells us, is a faculty of the soul. Our characters are forged of words in action flung out in a pattern of event. "It is not what we say, but how we say it," seems at first glance a shallow view of the art. Until we consider that allowing that "how" its will brings us to the heart of the fiction: the place where character-event-movement are charged.

What are we to understand of all this? I would say it depends what you mean by understand. What does God understand of us, his creatures? What do we understand of our characters and the things they do, and don't do, to, for, or in conjunction with one another?

When the person who was to introduce the first production of Beckett's *Waiting for Godot* asked him to explain a little about the play and the characters so that the audience would have a clue to understanding it, he said: "I know no more about the characters than what they say, what they do, and what happens to them... If I did manage to get slightly acquainted with them, it was only by keeping very far away from the need to understand."

Does this mean we are relieved from the burden of intellectual activity in moving our fictions forward? I would rather answer that by referring to the bicycle rider or tightrope walker obsessed with trying to understand how he managed to stay on the bike or on the wire, which of course caused him to fall off. Not because he tried to understand but because he reached for an imbalance — trying to understand with his mind that which was performed with his whole being — body, mind, heart, soul, holistically.

It's hard work, and we can never, as opposed to a painter, see the whole thing in a glance. A couple of summers ago, I had the privilege of spending two weeks in the chateau that used to be owned by Heinrich Maria Ledig-Rohwolt, the German publisher. It is now a writer's colony, Chateau Lavigny, and I was given the library to work in — a very large workroom on the floor of which I was able to fan out the hundred scenes of my novel-in-progress across the carpet so that I could scurry about on my knees trying to get an overview, to compare them, compare opening gambits, compare the very *look* of the text on the page, paragraph lengths, dialogue accumulations, etc.

But still, it is not the same as viewing a painting, can*not* be. A writer must inchworm his or her way through the work, even if it is just a short-story, perhaps even devising charts and maps to provide some semblance of overview, but mostly we can only *imagine* the whole thing — as one imagines an overview of the world we live in beyond the reaches of our vision, the town we live in, for example, which we can only really see in bits and pieces unless we turn to an aerial photograph, but that is such a *distant* view. We cannot see it all at once, close-up and far, from above and from within. Not even a Cubist can. Except in the imagination. And thus we are back to the imagination not only as a means of creating and of assembling, but as a way of knowing. Gordon Weaver illustrates the inevitability of the imagination with the analogy of the Big Dipper: "No dipper in the sky, but imagination allows us, maybe compels us to 'draw' the lines between the stars to form the dipper."

How are elements of the fiction selected and how are they to be understood? In some cases -- again, Hemingway's "Hills Like White Elephants," everything fits together perfectly, every detail *means* something specific, stands for something as surely as the symbols in a chemical formula — two characters on a train station in the middle of nowhere, to one side an arid field, to the other a fertile valley, and the hills beyond like the white elephants of children, and the reasonableness of the husband choosing the comfort offered by an abortion versus the unreasoned desire of the wife to procreate. How perfect, how terribly perfect, how dangerously close to the tautologies of an algebraic equation. Yet it works.

Other stories delineate ineffable mysteries, a puzzle for which the reader has to forge a key to unlock a fragment of contemplation that brings us *that* much closer to a vision of ourselves. Perhaps Hawthorne's "Young Goodman Brown," Melville's "Bartleby, the Scrivner," Andersen's "Death in the Woods," Flannery O'Connor's anything.

Remember Plato when he had Socrates say, "Not by wisdom do poets write poetry, but by a sort of genius and inspiration — they say many fine things but do not understand the meaning of them."

We — I — do imagine things for our fictions, but we also pick things up. If we're Tom Wolfe, we sit in a courtroom all day and take notes. The seashore of our days is scattered with experience like so many shells and feathers and stones that we gather and arrange in a collage.

Our fictions are full of esthetics, biogaphy, personal history, lies, imaginings, half-truths, pet citations, intimate revelations, scraps of conversation, the remembered flash of an eye, and the imaginative force that draws them all together into a tract that hangs together as a story.

As John Cheever put it: "You can pick and choose from a wide range of memory, picking the smell of roses from a very different place and the ringing of a tennis court roller that you heard years ago," and when a writer pushes open a fictional door to a fictional kitchen, he may well discover there a cook who had worked for his mother years before; and Cheever referred to this as "a confirmation of the feeling that life itself is creative process, that one thing is put purposefully upon another, that what is lost in one encounter is replenished in the next and that we possess some power to make sense of what takes place."

This, of course, is another way of speaking of what Coleridge called the esemplastic power of the imagination and the capability of forging unity out of diversity.

In Sherwood Andersen's story "Death in the Woods," from the 1930s, the narrator hears his older brother tell the story of a dead woman they saw in the woods and is not satisfied with the telling; he intuitively realizes the experience has a greater significance than is presented in the account his brother gives, so years later, he retells the event, embellishing it with details he has witnessed or heard of from other times and other places, to arrive at a very powerful story.

When the critic Irving Howe remarks that the meanderings in which the narrator explains where he has fetched these details from mar an otherwise excellent story, he misses the ball. The story is precisely about the way in which the process of art can find meaning in death.

I write by intuition, hoping in a sense, as Faulkner put it, to lie my way to the truth; I bring my mind to it later as Wordsworth spoke of poetry as the spontaneous overflow of emotion recollected in tranquility. But that process of recollection is for me always something of a fight with my mind. I let my intellect into the process as I might admit a dangerous animal into the circus of the fiction — it has its function there, it is powerful and wonderful, but an intellect, as a tiger, is also a dangerous carniverous beast and must be kept in check lest it play havoc in the garden, killing, driving all other living things into hiding.

I guess I write by intuition with an assist from the intellect. I guess I read pretty much the same way — only when reading, maybe I put down the whip and let the mind beast roam more freely. After all, he can't do much harm to the fiction I'm reading; it's already safely locked away upon the pages of a book.

How beautifully Rilke told it to the young poet:

"With nothing can one approach a work of art so little as with critical words; they always come down to more or less happy misunderstandings. Things are not all so comprehensible and expressible as one would mostly have us believe; most events are inexpressible, taking place in a realm which no word has ever entered, and more inexpressible than all else are works of art, mysterious existences, the life of which, while ours pass away, endures."

THE EUROPEAN AUTHORS WHO DESTROYED
THE ME WHO WAS DESTROYING ME

Among the background papers for a Danish literary
conference where I spoke not long ago was a chapter from a then
recent, very interesting book by Richard H. Pells entitled *Not
Like Us: How Europeans Have Loved, Hated and Transformed
American Culture Since World War II* (Basic Books, 1997). The
book addresses the interplay between American and European
literature in the 20th century. The conference background chapter
included the following statement:

"What really attracted (European) intellectuals, particularly
in Italy and France, to American fiction was the possibility that it
could help liberate them from the esthetic suffocation they felt in
their own countries."

As I understand it, this refers to the post-war years, and the
distinction is made, with particular reference to an interpretation
of Sartre's view that "a country as pragmatic as the U.S.
would...produce a literature better known for its technique than
its ideas." There is also mention of Camus trying to "mimic"
Hemingway in his novels.

Since I was educated by Dominican Nuns and Franciscan
and Irish Christian Brothers in the New York City boroughs of
Queens and Brooklyn and believed every word they told me, my
experience may be atypical, but that experience is the reverse of
what Mr. Pells suggests. It was European literature which
liberated me from the intellectual, esthetic, cultural, and sexual
suffocation I was experiencing in the United States in the 1950s

and early 60s.

Perhaps it was true in 1837 when Ralph Waldo Emerson said, "We have listened too long to the courtly muses of Europe," but it sounds to me more the statement of an adolescent breaking free — the country was just sixty years old at the time. But adolescents generally return to the collective wisdom after they have made their point and found their feet. And Andre Gide may, as Mr. Pells suggests, have admired the prose style of Dashiel Hammett, but I don't recall reading anything of Hammet's as profoundly moving as Gide's *Strait is the Gate*, say, or "The Pastoral Symphony." *The Maltese Falcon* is a merry chase and smacks of depth, but lacks I think the intense emotional power and honesty of Gide, who unlike Hammett has no use for melodrama. When I finished reading *Falcon*, I lit a butt and peered out the window into the foggy night feeling mighty pleased at the prospect of cobolt blue eyes out there somewhere; when I finished *Strait is the Gate*, I was devastated at the thought of lives wasted on spiritual misconceptions. Perhaps there are lives wasted on a misconception in *Falcon*, too, but it is a highly stylized one, dependent on melodrama, far less naturalistic I would say than the French writers of the period.

The United States for me, from the mid-50s to the early 60s, despite rock and roll, and Walt Whitman and the Beats notwithstanding (with all their wonderful modernist European roots), was a country in which the atmosphere was fraught with fear of the "danger on the edge of town" (as Jim Morrison put it in his heavily European-influenced rock performance, "The.End" in 1966). That danger was in the form of fear of communism and sexual "perversion." Bigotry, slurs against and authorized maltreatment of Negroes, Jews, Latin Americans and homosexuals were routine. Queer-bashing was, if not encouraged, fairly commonplace. I can recall my father telling about being in a bar where a man who was thought to be homosexual had a drink, following which the bartender picked up the empty glass and smashed it with a bat, saying, "There's a glass no man will have to touch his lips to." My father also told of carnivals he had been to as a boy where Negroes were hired to stick their heads through a hole in a tent so that people could, for a coin, throw a hardball at them.

And on the subject of *The Maltese Falcon*, how about the unabashed homophobic glee with which Humphry Bogart's Sam Spade smacks about Peter Lorre's Joel Cairo in the film version? The implication seemed to be that since Cairo is darkly foreign and effeminate he is slimy and a fit target for such treatment. "You'll take it and like it," Bogie tells him when he protests, for unlike Bogie, he is not a real, red-blooded, tough, whiskey-drinking, woman-kissing, fist-punching masculine American man.

In the U.S. of my adolescence, there was a general aversion to unshaven hair on a man's jaws and its suggestion of carnality and intellectualism. Men who wore sandals were feared and mocked. In fact, American Airlines in the sixties had a regulation against men wearing sandals without socks on their flights — although women could. And by the mid-60s, when some men had begun to wear their hair to their collars, this was enough to be curtly invited to leave a public establishment and, not uncommonly, to be physically attacked on the streets. I experienced this personally in New York and in Ohio, and my hair barely reached my collar.

It was literally illegal to display the naked human body in fact or photograph and, in most states, to fornicate outside of wedlock, commit adultery, masturbate, or in or out of wedlock to commit any act of so-called sodomy (the definition of which covered a multitude of acts today generally considered normal), or to print or publicly pronounce the famous four-letter word which describes the sound of the act which procreates human life.

As John Steinbeck stated in one of his books -- I think it was *Travels with Charley: In Search of America* from 1961 — there was a whole generation of American men who were intimate with the mechanics of the internal combustion engine and unaware of the existence of the clitoris. I recall reading that statement at the age of seventeen and having to go to my Webster for help.

How odd it seems now in retrospect that there was actually need for a movement at Berkeley in which students demonstrated wearing signs that read, "Fuck, Verb," in order to challenge (successfully so) these impossible laws and regulations. As the Finnish composer Einojuhani Rautavaara put it, "All taboos in art are a sort of myopia (in space or time) and often tantamount to racism."

Aristotle may have been correct that the word dog does not bite, but in 1964, the word 'fuck' could land you in jail and did — in the case of the comedian Lenny Bruce, for example, or the young San Francisco woman whose name I cannot recall but who published a poem entitled, "To Fuck with Love."

In 1952, the American expatriate writer (who has since assumed Irish citizenship) J. P. Donleavy returned from Dublin to New York to try to sell a novel he had completed titled *The Ginger Man*. New York editors, including John Hall Wheelock at Scribner's, were full of praise for the novel, but the publishing world was still unsettled over criticism of another recently published novel, James Jones's *From Here to Eternity*, and no one dared take on Donleavy's novel. It was not published in the United States in an unexpurgated version until 1965 — thirty-two years after a Random House editor had successfully fought to have lifted the ban on publishing James Joyce's *Ulysses*, a novel very much more sexually explicit than *The Ginger Man*.

In fact, the prefatory matter of my Random House edition of *Ulysses* includes not only the intelligent, courageous, praiseworthy text of the decision in 1933 by United States District Judge Woolsey to lift the ban on the novel, but also a letter to Bennet Cerf of Random House from James Joyce himself, thanking him for his "determination to fight for its legalisation in America."

I have to smile when I think of this. One of Bennet Cerf's other occupations was as a panelist on the American 50s/60s television game show *What's My Line?* My mother and father, God rest their loving souls, were great fans of that program and of Bennet Cerf and his corny puns. I can well remember Sunday evenings in the late 1950s sitting in the dark living room watching the grey light of the black and white teevee and still can see Mr. Cerf's grinning face, hear his snigger and his corny jokes.

We were devout Roman Catholics in my family. My father once burned a leather-bound set of the stories of Balzac for fear of scandalizing his children. In my teens when I learned about and objected to this book-burning, my father, with considerable embarrassment, explained to me the extent of Balzac's excess had left him no choice: "There was even a story in there," he whispered urgently to me, "about a man who went round in very tight britches and who could engorge his male organ at will and would do it in the presence of women to embarrass them!" I didn't have the guts to say, "So what!? That's funny!" Nor did I have the courage at a family dinner in 1963 or 64 to stand up for the comic erotic novel *Candy* which everyone was reading and I found brilliantly liberating and my family found shockingly appalling. No doubt Voltaire's *Candide*, a kindred classic , would have evoked a similar response had we read it.

I wonder now what my mother and father would have thought had they known that Bennet Cerf had fought to legalize Joyce's novel, one of whose main intents was to celebrate the same human body (let us not forget that each chapter of *Ulysses* is dedicated, inter alia, to a different organ of the human body) which the Catholic Church and other prudish American elements had fought hard and successfully to make us ashamed and frightened of — and which remained, in my experience, generally *un*freed by all of Walt Whitman's excellent songs of the body electric. (Actually Whitman, one of the great American innovators of the last century, smacks of controversiality in more than a few American communities today and perhaps the human body does, too.)

I recall in the last half of the fifties, sneaking up to the Earle Theater in Jackson Heights, located on a small alley-like side street known locally as "Fag Alley," to get a peek at the posters advertising European films. I recall one, Bergman it must have been, *One Summer of Happiness*, I think, which showed a man and woman standing waist deep in the ocean, naked, embracing. It was truly a picture of paradise for me at the age of fifteen, but a paradise scorned and feared by the world in which I lived. (Name me a public beach in the U.S. where a woman may freely bathe topless even today, in the 21st century! Where even an innocent child can go naked!)

In 1960, at the age of fifteen, some desperate sense of suffocation led me to raid my father's bookshelves. Despite what I have said earlier about the Roman Catholic colonization of my family's minds, my father was an avid reader, and he had many books. One sleepless night, I picked down *Crime & Punishment* by Feodor Dostoevski. My father had recommended it some time before. It did not help me sleep, for I sat up all night with it, and for several nights to come, and this experience marked the beginning of the development of my literary consciousness.

Nothing that we had read in school until then — and, let me give the Irish Christian Brothers their due, we read a good bit — struck me with the force of Dostoevski. For the remainder of that year and the two or three years to come I could not get enough of European writers. All of Dostoevski, Turgenev, Andre Gide, Francois Mauriac, Katherine Mansfield, Albert Camus, and finally, James Joyce, who quite completely deconstructed the bars of the cage around me, destroying the me who was destroying me.

Others would come a little later, Americans and Europeans and classical writers, but those few, primarily Dostoevski, Joyce, and Camus, effectively liberated my mind from the stranglehold of god, country, and repulsion from the human body.

I will never forget the power that entered my eighteen-year-old soul one winter night in 1962 as I sat on firewatch in a barracks in Fort Benjamin Harrison, Indiana, reading Camus's *The Stranger* and reached the point where M. Meursault, in his prison cell, took hold of the neckband of the priest's cassock, and shouted in his face, "All your certainties are not worth one strand of a woman's hair!"

It is the moment in the book when Meursault is freed from the prison of his own uncertainty, and at that moment in my life, had there been a leader there who called out to me to throw down my rifle and come and follow out into life, I think I would have done so.

Nothing in all of Hemingway has ever touched me with that power, and while I will grant that perhaps Camus's style took on some freedom from Hemingway's, there is no denying that there is a straight line from Søren Kierkegaard to that chapter in *The Stranger* — the scene in which Meursault learns of the leap of faith. If that is not European, I do not know what is, and it was in the form of those books that I found the way out of a country that was for me truly suffocating.

The coup de grâce to those strangling bonds was in Joyce's *Portrait of the Artist as a Young Man*:

> "You have asked me what I would do and what I would not do. I will tell you what I will do and what I will not do. I will not serve that in which I no longer believe, whether it call itself my home, my fatherland, or my church: and I will try to express myself in some mode of life or art as freely as I can and as wholly as I can, using for my defence the only arms I allow myself to use — silence, exile, and cunning."

This to me so clearly expressed the ideal of intellectual freedom that is the sign of a great civilization, and that civilization was in Europe, from which Joyce issued his proclamation. Compare with America's great offering, Hemingway, who came to learn the joys of European life and said:

> "I started out very quiet and I beat Mr. Turgenev. Then I trained hard and I beat Mr. de Maupassant. I've fought two draws with Mr. Stendahl, and I think I had an edge in the last one. But nobody's

going to get me in any ring with Mr. Tolstoy
unless I'm crazy or I keep getting better."
What *bull* in the afternoon!

In years to come, I would learn once again to love America and its people, to love the American way of openness and friendliness and helpfulness, but always now with a grain of uncertainty about a country unwilling or unable to construct a system that would ensure the degree of equality we see in many of the welfare systems of Europe. Don't get me wrong, I hate paying taxes, too, but I love the fact that in the so-called northern welfare states, for example, kids get comprehensive dental care, that everyone gets comprehensive medical care, that the school system right through the end of university, including medical school, is free of charge. In fact, students receive a modest salary while they study. And one wonders, against this backdrop, what Mr. John Irving is complaining about when he bemoans the fate of the unprotected minority of the rich.

Anyway, in the fifties, I too had come to notice, as Lawrence Ferlinghetti put it, "the close identification of the United States with the Promised Land where the coins all bear the words IN GOD WE TRUST, but the dollar bills do not have them, being gods unto themselves." Someone in the Treasury Department must have read Ferlinghetti's poem because they began putting those words on the bills then as well.

And speaking of bills, how arresting that in Ireland, where for decades, James Joyce was considered the antichrist incarnate, despised and unpublished, the ten pound note now bears his portrait along with a likeness of the Martello Tower from the opening scene of *Ulysses* and the first sentence of *Finnegans Wake*. In fact, as an Irish friend once showed me, if you turn the bill on its edge, the Martello Tower and the peninsula on which it is depicted bear an undeniable resemblance to an erect phallus: "That's what Molly Bloom's soliloquy was all about," my friend explained.

Also interesting that not long ago, a Dublin city project (no doubt funded by the European Union development fund) erected neon quotations from *Ulysses* around town — on the banks of the Liffy and such. One of them was from Molly Bloom's monologue and sat on the walls of Trinity College itself: It said, *I would not give one snap of my fingers for them and all their learning.* How sharply this contrasts with much of the public climate in the United States where politicians like Jesse Helms pit themselves against public support for the arts — and the fact that the United States is one of the few countries in the world which does not even have a Department of Culture. Why does the U.S. not want its artists and writers to challenge the status quo? Why are so many American publishers so meek and nervous?

The American culture has a treasure of its own, unequalled elsewhere in the world — its small publishers and literary magazines. This is a national treasure the likes of which do not exist elsewhere, and which the American people can and should be very proud of. However, the survival in these times of these houses and magazines is hand to mouth, life on the margin.

It interests me also to consider the fact that *The Stranger* was published in 1942, the same year that the not sufficiently known Irish poet Patrick Kavanagh (who died in 1967) published his amazing long narrative poem "The Great Hunger." That is not, as might be supposed, a poem about the potato famine, but about the starvation of the human heart and of passion. Shortly after the poem appeared, Kavanagh was visited by two large men, one of whom was holding a copy of the poem behind his back. Policemen. "Did you write this?" one of them demanded.

Of course I was far from alone banging against the walls of the bell jar four decades ago. Henry Miller had already been there long before, although his books were contraband. The Beats, too, were already there, driven by the engine of European modernism, and I would begin to discover them in the early to mid-sixties when the hippies appeared on the scene. But notwithstanding that Ginsberg's epigraph to *Howl* is from Whitman ("Unscrew the locks from the doors!/Unscrew the doors themselves from their jambs!") there was an immense European influence on the Beats, Dostoevski, Rimbaud, Baudelaire, Céline, Genet, etc., and Spengler's *Decline of the West* helped inspire their apocalyptic vision.

A fascinating two-volume anthology published in 1995 (*Poems for the Millenium, The University of California Book of Modern and Postmodern Poetry*, edited by Jerome Rothenberg and Pierre Joris, University of California Press) affords a stunning overview of the late nineteenth and early twentieth century esthetics that have contributed to the evolution of our consciousness. And apart from Whitman, Dickinson, Stein, Pound, and Eliot (the latter three expatriates), by far the main influence is European — Hölderlin, Lönnrot, Baudelaire, Hopkins, Rimbaud, Mallermé, Cavafy, Rilke, Appolinaire, Kafka... Hundreds of them.

As Mallermé said, "I have news for you, verse has been tampered with."

Many European academics of my generation or even of the generation following mine will argue that their youth was equally confined by closed-mindedness, by sexual and intellectual repression, by the constraints of dead or dying traditions. One may ask, for example, How many Danes have actually read Kierkegaard? Or how many Europeans — or Americans — have actually read *Ulysses*? Even if the book — whose author never won a Nobel prize — was named in a recent survey among the top 100 novels of this century (in the United States it was named number one, while in the United Kingdom it was named number 100).

Yes, yes, and yes. As the wonderful American story writer John Cheever was fond of saying, "Literature is not a competitive sport," and of course it is not (Ernest Hemingway and Norman Mailer notwithstanding). For every European writer I can point to who helped me, as a young person and a young writer, out of the maddening airless room of chauvinism, one can name any number of Americans as well. For Gogol there is Hawthorne; for Doestoevski, Melville. For every great American jazz musician who was sheltered from American persecution in France or Scandinavia, there was an East European novelist sheltered in America from Bolshevik oppression.

The real literary world perhaps is a single, universal one which knows no real boundaries of time or nation. It goes back some five thousand years to *The Epic of Gilgamesh* and continues on through the Egyptians and the Greeks and the Bible, the Romans, all the old myths and epics, and on up to Chaucer, Boccaccio, Shakespeare, Cervantes, Pascal, Descartes...

Well, no need to recite the entire cannon.

As I sit writing this essay it is the end of an early spring day, and I gaze out over my computer through the window that looks out onto one of the lakes bordering the edge of the center of Copenhagen. At this very moment, on the path along the lake a young man and woman pause, strolling past, to kiss, then continue on. The path they walk on is known as *Kærligheds Stien* (The Love Path). It is the same path that the main character of Søren Kierkegaard's *The Diary of a Seducer* walked in 1843, peering north across the water toward the object of his desire.

The water is blue and pink, the branches of the chestnuts on the bank sit like scratchwork against the Copenhagen sky, and I consider the fact that my eighteen year old daughter is considering a major in philosophy in college. For my fifty-fifth birthday earlier that month she gave me a copy of Ludwig Wittgenstein's *Philosophical Investigations*, saying, "Dad, I heard you say the other day that you never actually read Wittgenstein. Now you can." And my son, who had been wavering between a major in history or literature, made his decision after seeing Polanski's *Macbeth*: "English," he said. "That language!" And the two of them receive a state salary and attend a university that charges no tuition — as do all university students in Denmark. With our taxes, we buy civilization, as Oliver Wendell Holmes put it; apparently half the American people, if the Republican platforms are any measure, are not interested in buying civilization.

On the water of the lake a duck swims toward the shore beneath my window, the V of its wake spreading wide behind it. On my desk is a framed photograph of myself flanked by my children on a bridge in Venice, beside that is one of Edna St. Vincent Millay, one of my father's favorite poets, beside that one of Langston Hughes smiling at his desk in Harlem in 1954, when I was ten years old across the East River in Queens and had not yet heard of him, beside that one of Thomas Wolfe boarding a trolly in Munich in the 1930s, and beside that one of the stone angel that adorns his grave — an angel brought from Italy to Ashford, North Carolina, by his father nearly a hundred years ago — an angel that would inspire the title of his wonderful novel, *Look Homeward, Angel*.

A stone, a leaf, an unfound door. A dream deferred vindicated in its enunciation.

Our world is a continuum. It is one world made up of many parts, the spirit of each nourishing the spirit of the other with that which is needed to maintain the balance of this splendid privilege of existence.

REALISM & OTHER ILLUSIONS

"If you want to give a natural appearance to an imaginary creature, a dragon for example, use the head of a mastiff or a pointer, the eyes of a cat, the ears of a hedgehog, the snout of a hare, the smile of a lion, the temples of a cock, and the neck of a tortoise."
                        -Leonardo da Vinci

"If people see a lion, they run away; if they only apprehend a deduction, they keep wandering round in an experimental humor. Now how is the poet to convince like nature, and not like books?"
                        -Robert Louis Stevenson

When we read a piece of fiction, what is it about the work that inspires the "willing suspension of disbelief" that Coleridge identified as necessary to the experience of literature? What makes us willing, even eager to believe that the artificial world into which the writer invites us is a real one? The problem may not be so acute with realistic works — if we pick up a book and begin to read, for example,

"The Jackman's marriage had been adulterous and violent, but in its last days, they became a couple again, as they might have if one of them were slowly dying."

we accept the premise immediately. With this opening to his story, "The Winter Father," Andre Dubus fills us in on the essence of a compelling situation which we automatically place in a setting in the real world, and he goes on to tell skillfully a moving story about the dissolution of family life which is or was so central to the short story of the eighties and nineties.

Likewise, we react with belief when we read the opening of Raymond Carver's "Collectors."

"I was out of work. But any day I expected to hear from up north. I lay on the sofa and listened to the rain. Now and then I'd lift up and look through the curtain for the mailman."

The scene is not unfamiliar. It is set with objects familiar to us, simple actions that we know from our own experience, charged subtly with emotions that we ourselves have experienced or could easily imagine experiencing.

Gladys Swan opens her novel *Carnival for the Gods* like this:

"It was the first time Dusty had ever backhanded her, and it was not just the blow, the pain, the blood from her lip flowing saltily into her mouth that gave Alta the shock: it was the sense that something fatal had struck at the roots of her life."

Again, a situation sufficiently grounded in recognizably real detail to be accepted without trouble as reality, as is this opening of Francois Camoin's story, "Lieberman's Father":

"Lieberman had his eyes on his chicken salad and so at first didn't see the woman. She stopped short at his table and stood swaying a little this way and that, looking like a person who has just bumped into something and is wondering if she's hurt herself."

Such openings seem immediately real enough, "normal"

enough not to raise questions in our minds about where they are happening. They seem to be happening in the same world we occupy, and we accept them as such. But sometimes they seem to nudge toward the border of another dimension. Here's how Gordon Weaver's "The Interpreter" starts:

> "It is as if... It is as if I cannot remember the things I must say to myself. It is as if all the words I know in both English and my native Mandarin have fled from me, evaporated into the cold, misty air of this wretched place, into the wet fogs that greet us each morning... It is as if each bitter day is the first and I wake chilled...knowing nothing until I can remember some words, something to say to myself that will allow me to rise."

Not *un*realistic, yet there is an edge of the other there that makes us a little unsure just where we are.

And what is one to make of a short story from *Leaf Storm* by Gabriel Garcia Márquez that opens with a character named Palayo walking home from the beach, entering his courtyard to find "a very old man, lying face down in the mud" and unable to rise because "his enormous wings" are in the way? How are we to suspend our disbelief and enter Márquez's world — even if we desperately want to?

Or the opening of Robert Coover's story "Beginnings":

> "In order to get started, he went to live alone on an island and shot himself. His blood, unable to resist a final joke, splattered the cabin wall in a pattern that read: It is important to begin when everything is already over."

How are we to be encouraged or enabled to incorporate the conditions of that bizarre world into our own experience?

All of the examples given above can be grouped into two different categories which differ from each other in one basic manner of narrative strategy. The first five examples (Dubus,

Carver, Swan, Camoin, Weaver) being in more or less clear "realistic" modes, invite us into a world which from the start presents itself as part of the world we automatically would assume to be the setting of any occurrence related to us, be it fiction or nonfiction. The setting, we assume, is *our* world, *here*, where we live, or at least in some other land that really exists and can be "seen" in the atlas. With Weaver, we are a little uncertain where we are, and with an opening like Márquez's or Coover's, we know that the setting is not a "real" one, that the "place" in which the story occurs would seem rather to be located somewhere in the imagination than in the external world.

How, then, is the writer to persuade us of the "reality" of what he is reporting in a manner as though it is really occurring or has occurred? How does the author succeed in making us read on, in suspending our disbelief?

It is important to recognize that all of the above examples are examples of illusion, whether the illusion is a realistic one, a surrealistic one, a superrealistic one, or a so-called fabulist, metafictional, or postmodern one. It was the French novelist Émile Zola who said, "The realists of art should really be called the illusionists." Or as Robert Louis Stevenson put it over a hundred years ago, in a review of Walt Whitman's *Leaves of Grass*: "This question of realism, let it be then clearly understood, regards not in the least degree the fundamental truth, but only the technical method of a work of art."

While the overall technique or strategy may vary, the basic trick, the basic illusion, is generally pretty much the same, what is called verisimilitude — from the Latin *verisimilitudo* — or *verus similis* — *verus* (true) and *similis* (similar), or the French *vrai semblance* —- that is, something which has the appearance of being true or real, something which *seems* to be true or plausible or likely. Some theorists, like John Gardner, hold the use of verisimilitude to mean that the writer evokes in a large sense, a "true likeness" of the world in which we live — which harkens back to Aristotle's mimetic theory of art put forth in his *Poetics*, that art imitates or mirrors life — but this seems to me too narrow a view of the concept and, ultimately, one that cannot hold, for *no* writer of fiction, not even the most realistic, not even the superrealists, the Edward Hoppers or Duane Hansens or Kurt Trampedach's of prose, fashions a "true likeness" of the world in the largest sense. Have you ever noticed that in Hopper's wonderful evocative portraits of the city there is never any rubbish in the street? All manner of distortion, selection, rearrangement of facts and details is necessary in the writing of fiction. Therefore, I hold to the interpretation of the concept of verisimilitude as merely the creation of an imaginary universe which seems to be real, and that all writers of fiction seek to create an imaginary universe which seems to be real via the use, either continual or occasional, of verisimilitude.

What is verisimilitude? My definition is this: Verisimilitude is that quality of a work of fiction by which a physical, psychological, and spiritual reality is rendered such that the reader is persuaded to suspend disbelief in order that the author's creative discovery regarding existence may be explored and experienced by the reader.

How can this concept apply to the last two examples given above? Márquez and Coover? How can such pieces be given the appearance of reality, most specifically of a physical reality?

As Flannery O'Connor says, "Fiction begins where human knowledge begins — with the senses." We have only five ways of perceiving reality: we can see it, hear it, taste it, smell it, touch it. Or in the case of fiction, we can *seem* to do these things.

Let's look at how Marquez does this with the old man with wings. How does he make us believe in this? First of all, he is lying in the mud, about as vivid and clearly grounded an image as can be found. If he appeared flying above Palayo's head, or seated on a cloud with a harp and wearing immaculate white linen, our doubt might be so much stronger, but when we see the mud on the old angel's face, he has been brought down to earth and our senses begin to respond, our perception of our senses, and as we read on we learn that this old man has very few teeth in his mouth and that "his huge buzzard wings" are "dirty and half-plucked." As we get even closer, we learn further that the old angel has "an unbearable smell," and that the backs of his wings are infested with lice! This Márquez, we begin to feel, he knows his angels! By now the reader has seen and smelled this creature and has shivered at the sight of the lice chewing at the spotty pink chicken flesh of his wings, and this preposterous bizarre creature has been admitted into our imagination by Gárcia's brilliant use of verisimilitude — the replica of that which our senses can perceive, even if only the imaginary counterparts of our senses perceiving the imagined aspects of an image.

Thus, Márquez has shocked us out of our normal expectations of reality, only to coax us back in again by manipulating our senses, turning them against our skepticism. We are made to *smell* the universe being painted in the sky for us. How can you deny the existence of something that *stinks*? "Creations of the mind," Baudelaire said, "are more alive than matter."

Interestingly, though, if we look further at some of the so-called "realistic" examples given above — let's pick Camoin and Swan — we will find a strategy which is very much the reverse of that used by the Márquez example given.

In the Camoin story, we follow a half page of fairly ordinary realistic description. The woman speaks to the man at the table, addresses him by his name. He does not recognize her, asks how she could know his name, and she tells him he'll have to prepare himself for a shock. "This won't be easy for you," she says. She asks permission to sit down, to drink a glass of water, and then she tells him, "I am your father."

He answers, "I already have a father," and she says, "I am your real father." And the remainder of this realistic story deals with the main character dealing with this incomprehensible, impossible, unreal, paradoxical, yet somehow intriguing, compelling situation of a man being accosted by a woman who claims to be his real father. Camoin snares us in a realistic trap into following an impossible situation in which he creates a reality that defies the natural laws — or at the very least the terminology — we have come to know and trust in our own "real" world. Bertold Brecht: "Art is not a mirror held up to reality, but a hammer with which to shape it."

Similarly, Gladys Swan's realistic story begins with something about as real and concrete as can be: a smack in the mouth, a cut lip, the taste of blood on the tongue. We know that pain, discomfort of running the edge of the tongue over a sore inside the lip, the salt taste of blood, and we are with her at once. But that story turns out to be the first chapter of a novel in which the world she will lead us into will become more and more strange, surreal, a world which is deep within the imagination the deeper we follow. But we *do* follow because she has made us taste the blood of her world, "proving" its existence to us, coaxing us in by realistic details in a somewhat similar way that fairy tales do. As Bruno Bettelheim points out in his book *The Uses of Enchantment: On the Interpretation of Fairy Tales*, fairy tales "usually start out in a quite realistic way: a mother telling her daughter to go all by herself to visit grandmother..." as the beginning of a series of increasingly mythical, symbolic, and often terrifying occurrences.

Interesting comparisons and contrasts can be made between the ways in which Swan employs verisimilitude and the ways it is used by Gordon Weaver and by Andre Dubus in their stories. Weaver, in his story collection *A World Quite Round*, employs essentially realistic narrative in a variety of ways that veer across realism's borders into regions of intentional anti-illusionism, where he discusses the illusions he is creating and, ironically, in the process, creates an even stronger illusion — that of the truth speaker who destroys illusions. Or else he constructs a kind of shadow story exploring the nature of the language in which the story is told — as with his novella "The Interpreter." Or he deals subtly with the creation of art in general and its relation to identity and existence as in his story "Ah Art! Oh Life!"

In virtually all of Andre Dubus's stories, he has sought his metaphors and meanings in the daily experiences of the lives of his characters in a realism which aims as nearly as possible to imitate a reality experienced by real people in a real world.

But what all these examples have in common is that by manipulating the details of physical or sensory "reality" of the fictional world, the writer creates a dimension to house its psychological and spiritual reality as well: Coover's linguistic island where death is the beginning and blood writes sentences on the wall, Swan's carnival, Weaver's world of language, Camoin's paradox, but also the psychological or spiritual reality of a world like our own, as in the work of Dubus, Carver, and all the other "realists" of our time.

The use of so-called particulars in fiction — objects, sensory impressions — serves more than one purpose; at one and the same time, it enables the writer to create a realistic and a magical world. Alice McDermott says, "We use detail in fiction to tame time, to step on life's receding tail. We use precise detail...not merely because it makes for better, more vivid writing; we use detail because the moment of conscious contact holds a drop of solace."

Thus, the physical detail at once stops time, comforts the reader, and bolsters the realistic illusion. But it does more, it infuses that illusion of reality with magic: "The moment an object appears in a narrative," says Italo Calvino, "it is charged with a special force and becomes like the pole of a magnetic field, a knot in the network of invisible relationships. The symbolism of an object may be more or less explicit, but it is always there. We might even say that in a narrative any object is always magic."

A friend of mine came home from work one day to find his Colombian mother-in-law sitting at his dining table trying to glue together the pieces of one of his favorite vases.

"What happened to it?" he asked. She looked up at him and explained, "A bat flew in the window and knocked it over." His mother-in-law was neither crazy nor stupid, but she had a rich Colombian imagination — her only mistake was in not realizing the sad depths of skepticism and shallowness of imagination of her North American neighbors. In Colombia, I imagine, this explanation of the broken vase would evoke a glimmering aura of magical connections, meanings, interpretations; in New York, it called forth nothing but an unvoiced if amused accusation: "What bullshit."

Psychological and spiritual verisimilitude will also be achieved via the recording of a fictional character's private perceptions — as when Alta, smacked in the mouth by her husband, experiences a sense of danger having entered the roots of her existence.

Such use of verisimilitude to suspend disbelief of a world existing in whole or part beyond the world of the senses, per se, created in a dimension only of sensual *image* or imitation, also calls to mind Hawthorne's definition of fiction as "a neutral territory somewhere between the real world and fairyland where the actual and imaginary may meet and each imbue itself with the nature of the other" and Melville's reference to it as exhibiting "more reality than real life itself can show." Saul Bellow, in *Humboldt's Gift*, performs an amusing and effective reversal, rendering a woman character "real" with a reference to art, by saying she had teeth "like the screaming horse in Picasso's *Guernica*."

Earlier I mentioned John Gardner's view of the concept of verisimilitude — his conception that a fiction of verisimilitude was a wholly realistic one meant to be experienced as occurring in the imagined reflection, if you will, of the world in which we find ourselves — recalling Aristotle's mimetic theory of art. Even Chekhov challenges this when the black monk, in his remarkable story of that title, says, "I exist in your imagination, and your imagination is part of nature which means that I exist in nature, too."

In contrast to Gardner's theory, we have theories such as

Jerome Klinkowitz's in *The Practice of Fiction in America*, which refers to the mimetic theory of art as "voodoo," an attempt to substitute the ficiton for what is real.

Alain Robbe-Grillet has said, "...academic criticism in the West as in the communist countries, employs the word 'realism' as if reality were already entirely constituted...when the writer comes on the scene. Thus it supposes that the latter's role is limited to 'explaining' and 'expressing' the reality of his period." This, in opposition to the view of fiction as *creative of reality* — Brecht's hammer, Kafka's axe to chop away the ice of our frozen consciousness.

So now we are back to the question of whether not only "realism" but reality itself is a fiction forged of the language in which it is expressed.

It is interesting to think of this in relation to some examples of political propaganda. Following the troubles in the People's Republic of China in 1989, the Chinese Government began issuing a series of booklets whose aim clearly was to write the history of the events in Tiananmen Square. As they put it in one of their press releases, "At present...many people are not clear about the truth. Therefore, there is a need to explain the truth about the counter-revolutionary rebellion..."

There is a wild beauty in the raging naivete of this which makes me think of some of the tarter fictions of Donald Barthelme where one is hypnotized by statements of blatant paradox: "She comes to him fresh from the bath, opens her robe. 'Goodbye,' she explains, 'Goodbye.'"

One of my favorite of the Chinese propoganda booklets is the one titled "How Chinese View the Riot in Beijing," in which the anonymous propaganda writer composes a number of fictional personas and has them present their "view" of what happened. For example, there is one titled "An Old Worker on the Riot" which begins,

> "I am an ordinary old worker. In the recent period when I saw our sacred and solemn

Tiananmen Square become a scene of great disorder and confusion, a filthy place that gave off a strong smell, I felt as if a fire were burning in my heart. In those days, a gang of counter-revolutionary thugs made unbridled attacks on the Chinese Communist Party..."

Clearly a case of political coopting of the fictional technique of realism, verisimilitude, and persona to present a fabricated version of reality, an illusion.

An even more bizarre example can be found in *The Medical Profession and Human Rights Handbook* (New York and London: Zed Books with British Medical Association, 2001) in its exposé of arguments used to support capital punishment by lethal injection via the following summary of a Chinese newspaper report from February 1999:

Four individuals had been sentenced to execution on 4 November 1997 and (when they) were told the day before that lethal injection would be used... 'they rejoiced greatly.' During the execution a doctor reportedly asked one of the condemned how it felt. He responded that 'it's good, it doesn't hurt.' It took between 32 and 58 seconds for the men to die.

Of course, the West too uses fictional technique in its propaganda. Amongst my collection, I have a nice sleek booklet entitled, *Ladies and Gentlemen: The 41st President of the United States*, distributed by the United States Information Service immediately after George Bush (the father) was elected and which also seems aimed at the creation of a fictional persona:

George took after his ebullient and empathetic mother. He liked pleasing people. 'He was the easiest child to bring up,' his mother says, 'very obedient.' The Bushes competed at everything — golf, tennis, tiddlywinks — anything that measured one person against another... The

concept of family was so powerful that it
sometimes seemed to friends that the Bush
children functioned as a single mind rather than as
five kids fighting for parental affection."

That single mind concept is kind of scarey — like science fiction, and the concept that a tiddlywinks match measures one person against another... One thinks of Hemingway's imagined fistfights with great European authors of the past.

It works the other way, too. *The Starr Report* investigation into the "Nature of President William Jefferson Clinton's Relationship with Monica Lewinski" reads very much like anti-realism, rather like a postmodern fiction by Harold Jaffe or Robley Wilson, Jr., or Donald Barthelme in which intimate detail is narrated in such rigid prose that it begins to seem surreal or even irreal.

In his fascinating book *Fiction and the Figures of Life*, William H. Gass comments on the mimetic theory of fiction by pronouncing pathetic the view of fiction as creative of living persons rather than of mere characters by pointing out that fiction is made out of words and words only. "It is shocking really," he says, to realize this — rather like discovering after all those years "that your wife is made of rubber."

In *The Art of Fiction*, John Gardner says, "In any piece of fiction, the writer's first job is to convince the reader that the events he recounts really happened...or might have happened (given small changes in the laws of the universe)...The realistic writer's way of making events convincing is verisimilitude." Gardner says that the tools of verisimilitude are "actual settings (Cleveland, San Francisco, Joplin, Missouri), precision of detail...streets, stories, weather, politics, etc., and plausible behavior."

As an example, Gardner names the question, "Would a mother really say that?" — a question he claimed to pose every time a mother in fiction speaks. However, if we look at a piece called "The Philosophers" by Russel Edson, we read this opening:

"I think, therefore I am, said a man whose mother
quickly hit him on the head saying, I hit my son
on his head, therefore I am..."

According to Gardner's formula, we are obliged to ask
ourselves, "Would a mother really say that?"

Well, I don't know, yes and no, she might not *say* it, she
might just thump him on the head, actually or metaphorically,
without explaining the importance of doing so for her own
existential identity. Perhaps it presents a deeper level of reality of
her behavior, of the relationship between son and mother, of
human modes of existential identification. In other words, a
mother might or might not actually say and do such a thing, but
one recognizes immediately that this is not the point, that a reality
is being presented via details that *could* occur, even if they are
absurd, and thus here exists verisimilitude: we have a son, a
mother, action, speech. A son speaks, is hit, answered. It *could*
have happened. We laugh or curl our toes. it is absurd, but it is
also true, reveals a hidden reality in a very efficient manner, and
really it doesn't matter at all whether it ever happened or is meant
to have happened: we have followed Edson into a dimension of
the imagination as surely as when we follow Alice through the
looking glass.

Russel Edson is good at this sort of thing:

Father throws the baby in the air. The baby hits
the ceiling. Stop, says mother, the ceiling is
crying, you're hurting the ceiling.

Would a mother really say that? Well, it is not inconceivable
that some mother at some time whose little boy runs headlong
into her Louis Quartorze writing table and falls bleeding profusely
from the scalp upon her 19th century Persian carpet may have
been heard to scream "Oh God" My poor table! My beautiful
carpet! You clumsy fool!" That, too, is a kind of verisimilitude
in certain cases.

"A bat flew in the window and knocked it over." Would a
mother-in-law really say that? I have only my friend's word for it,

but I believe it; even if it is a lie, I believe it.

Of course, it all comes down to the question, What is real? To many people, life sometimes seems little more than a series of repetitions of meaningless events: we rise, we eat, we go to work, we come home again, we eat, look at the tube, sleep, rise again, etc. If that is what our lives really have become, a story like Robert Coover's "The Elevator" — written in rebellion against standard realism and the conventional view of an orderly reality, and depicting a series of scenes of a man entering his office building each day to ride up to his office and the adventures he experiences during those few minutes, each scene a kind of parody of a literary style — is perhaps more realistic than surrealistic, even though the events depicted are far from conventional ones and the intention is perhaps more theoretical than representational.

Perhaps such a fiction employs verisimilitude to portray an "unreal" world that reflects something more essential of contemporary existence than a story built on linear plot and movement in which a meaningful progression of events is depicted, leading from beginning through complication of logical occurrences and cause and effect to a climax and resolution.

Jimmy Carter, nearly thirty years ago, looked directly into a television camera and, imagining the American public before him, said, "I want you to listen carefully now. I will never tell you a lie."

Applying John Gardner's verisimilitude test to that, we may ask ourselves, Would an American President really say that? But he did, just as William Jefferson Clinton, two decades later, would look into a nationwide camera and pronounce, "I did *not* have sexual relations with that woman." Where Carter's statement was perhaps a mere well-meant but naive and self-deluding pronouncement, Clinton's would later show itself to be a postmodernistic manipulation of language of breathtaking skill.

The illusion is always in the language. Add two or three words to Al Gore's statement about inventing the internet — say, "early fostered the *idea* of" — and the result is interest instead of scorn; just as when young Dubya Bush refers to Greeks as "Grecians," with one word he creates the unshakeable image of a man abysmally ill-informed in international affairs.

Unlike Jimmy Carter and like Bill Clinton, a fiction writer must select, manipulate, eliminate, foreshorten, lie — and he must do it in the interests of a truth greater than what can be found in our confusing everyday reality. A writer may lie by seeming to duplicate reality or by seeming to destroy it — the anti-illusionist we see at work for example in John Barth's *The Floating Opera* and *Lost in the Funhouse.* Barth begins *The Floating Opera* by having his first person creative narrator tell the reader that he has never written a novel before but has read a few to try to get the hang of it — immediately convincing the reader, duping him, into believing that this is not fiction, but a straight-from-the-heart account. Anti-illusion becomes in this way an even stronger illusion.

Most readers probably don't give much thought to the fact that the prounoun "I" in a fiction almost always is every bit the fictional persona as the pronoun "he" or "she," a created character, a mask the author holds before his or her face as the actors did in Greek tragedies. This is a concept Robert Pinsky professes to be liberated of: "When I say <u>I</u> (in a poem), I mean whatever it is that I mean when I say <u>I</u> in speaking to you. The poem is something that Robert says — that is not to say that Robert is, in my mind, a stable entity...in a sense, persona and archetype are not any more conditions of literature than they are of life for me...the idea of persona...was in style when I was in college; one of the great liberating and enabling moments for me was when i was able to decide I wasn't going to pay attention to it."

This is an interesting approach; however, for most fiction writers, I am convinced it applies to no extent greater than that which applied to Flaubert when he said, *"Madame Bovary, c'est moi."*

And one can scarcely avoid the fact that, for example, writing a story with a first person child narrator necessarily limits the author's use of language and observational sophistication while the same story in third person could bear the expression of a more mature consciousness to relate the child's story, with the child's sensibility cast into a richer, more mature language. The same effect, of course, can be achieved in first person with a time distance, a moment of narration cast well into the future, but this only further illustrates the fact that the personal pronoun I is rarely a simple matter.

"I, *I*! ...the filthiest of all the pronouns," said Carlo Emilio Gadda. "They are the lice of thought. When a thought has lice, it scratches, like everyone with lice...and in your fingernails, then...you find pronouns: the personal pronouns."

On the matter of dogmatic realism in fiction, when Ezra Pound complained to James Joyce that *Finnegans Wake* was obscure, Joyce answered, "Well now, Ezra, the action of my work takes place at night. It is natural, isn't it, that things should not be so clear at night?"

We have probably all seen spy films in which the action at night is so realistically depicted that we are left completely in the dark as to what is happening. The point is, we don't have to *use* darkness to fictionalize the dark. We use words, impressions, and our aim in fiction is to elucidate the deeper reality of darkness, not to reproduce a sensation of being in the dark for the sake of that sensation alone.

I believe that an examination of virtually every fictional mode will show that verisimilitude is an element at work in all of them, that in a large sense all fiction writers are "realists," in that all are dealing with reality.

Realism is only one of a number of available artistic illusions, all of which depend for their plausibility on some measure of verisimilitude.

In Gladys Swan's novel *Carnival for the Gods*, a carnival

illusionist, a sleight-of-hand "artist" who, in popular terms, is known as a "magician," is approached by a boy who believes the man's magic to be real and who asks to be taught the secrets of that art. The man is so unnerved by the boy's faith in magic that he lies to him and pretends that he *can* teach magic to the child in hopes that he will divert the boy from falling into evil secrets.

But the boy is undaunted. When, finally, the illusionist dies, the boy still believes that he can find what he seeks. He takes the dead magician's cape and goes off on his own, determined to search for what he seeks and, in the closing words of the book, "if he didn't find it, to create it in an imagined land."

I find this a concise and powerful summary of the process of art. Wrapped in the mantle of a fake circus magician, the artist sets out to imagine a land in which truth can be created.

For the fiction writer, verisimilitude is the tool of the imaginative act by which that truth is sought, the soil in which an imaginary garden can grow and provide a home for the toads of that which is genuine.

And it is the same for the realist and for the innovator, the experimenter, the task is the same. All is permitted.

NOSES IN FICTION

"*Tout est bien sortant des mains
de l'Auteur des choses.*"
  -Rousseau

"While out walking, he met a beggar all covered in
sores. His eyes were glazed, the end of his nose
was eaten away, his mouth was askew, his teeth
black, and he spoke from the back of his throat.
He was racked by a violent cough and spat out a
tooth with every spasm."
  -Voltaire, *Candide*

*I raise my fingers like a levitator, lower them into position,
close my eyes, wait — a passive instrument of creation.*

"Today," the professor said, "we shall be discussing noses in
fiction. This, you may well imagine, if you stop to imagine, is a
highly specialized topic. For practically no one in fiction has a
nose."

A young woman at the center of the classroom stood up and
began to undress.

"Young lady," said the professor, standing behind his desk,
pressing his fly against the edge of wood, "please stop that."

The young woman, who was tall and unnaturally thin, had
already removed her blouse. She was wearing a brassiere, although

she was without breasts. The white cups were empty, sunken. She turned her face up to the professor, who gasped. The young lady had no nose. Where a nose should have been was blank.

The professor closed his eyes. He felt dizzy, felt himself on the edge of the precipice, the nudging hand beginning to fondle his sleeve. The young woman — was she *real*?

(Question for study: what is the meaning of the word "real" when used of a character in a fiction?)

Who, in fact, was present in the room? Was anything there at all beyond the red-black curtain of his eyelids? Or was he alone, sealed into the envelope of his own solitary madness? Did the room have doors? Windows? Were there paintings on the walls? A light overhead? How many students had been present?

What existed?

What was *real*? (That word again.)

He opened his eyes and spoke: "*It is as if there is nothing, no shape, no texture, no sense, unless and until I find some words that will enable me to begin again. For fiction is made of words, and merely words. Shocking really. It is as though you had discovered that your wife were made of rubber. After all those years.* Nothing exists here until it is framed, forged in words."

"What a hunka horseshit," muttered a burly, bearded young man slung low in a chair by the window.

"Ah!" said the professor. "There! Now! You see? You, young man, now exist only as a function of the seventeen words in the preceding paragraph! As to whether or not the unnaturally thin young woman with neither nose nor breasts exists as a 'real' creature or not is held in abeyance for the moment, for I have questioned her 'reality' and have not yet dealt definitively with the question. The question is, of course, absurd, *n'est-ce pas*? For she cannot be real. She is a fiction. She is no realer than one of Munch's howling mouths, for example. One of Hundertwasser's warped houses. No realer than a piece of math, say. A hunk of philosophy. She is *not* a person. Cannot be. She is a fiction. Therefore, the real question is does she conform to the norm of reality created or *implied* as the functioning base upon which this fiction is to unfold itself?"

"Whatta buncha *crap*!" muttered the bearded young man by the window. "*You're* not the author, jerk-off."

"*I*," the professor pronounced with a quiet smile, "am very close to the heart of the author. And I do not mean the implied author either. I mean the *author*."

"Shove Wayne C. Booth up your anus, if you've been given one, Gass-face."

(Question for study: Who said that? You, dear reader, assume that the bearded young man did, don't you? But the quote is not attributed, it hangs there in midspace without a trace of the fictional mouth which is purported to have uttered it. The exclamation point indicates it has been exclaimed, the quotation marks that it has 'actually' been said, for in fiction only things 'actually' spoken earn quotes, all else being given instead in italics unless quotes are used to underscore the 'wordness' of a word or its limited applicability under a special situation — e.g., referring to an 'actual' event or 'real' person within a fiction, as opposed, say, to a 'ghost'. Thus, the exclamation in question has 'actually' been exclaimed, according to the conventions. That much we must be able to rely upon — otherwise the whole game is out. But exclaimed by whom?)

"I shall tell you by whom," said the professor, glancing from the page at his author, gazing up into the infinite beckoning depths of dark cavernous nostrils hovering up above the keyboard of the Acer travelmate 515Te that was wordprocessing him.

(He is right, the author thought, he is very close to me. Just see how I let him speak to me directly. God, my own author, would never let me do that to Him. My God! he thought with sacrilegious agitation, perhaps I am a kinder god than God, Himself, my own Author!)

(But who is this author we see thinking here? Is it, in

*fact me? Can it be? For once I am present in the fiction,
I too become a fiction, only an implication framed in
words, a narrative persona, while the real author, like
God, Himself, can be viewed only via the product of his
creation, and the view is always equivocal and
contradictory.*)

"How about you knock off the schizophrenic-like asides
now," the professor suggested, "and let me get on with my
business here?"

I shall decide what your so-called business here is, my friend.

"I warn you," the professor said. "hold the rein too tight and
you'll choke me to death."

*Tell it to E. M. Forster, wimp. I can well understand if his
characters mutinied on that tedious passage to India. My characters
are gally-slaves. They do as they are told by my words. For words are
all they are.*

The professor rapped the desktop before him with his
knuckles. "Yet the fact remains. *You* do not know who made the
exclamation nine paragraphs above, do you?"

I must confess I do not. And what of it?

"Nor do you always know what your words are going to do.
In fact, if you *try* to make them do something, they desert you.
You have no power over words, not really. Try to think
something in words. You can't, can you? You can only wait for
them to shape your thought."

*Nonetheless, I have created you. And if I wished I could
crumple you up and pitch you out.*

"I would live on in the trash."

Right. Trashily.

"I would haunt your creative thoughts."

*I would drown you in a double vodka, turn you into a woman,
dream up other interesting adventures to discourage your presence.*

"Are you quite certain you would *ever* be free of me?

*Perhaps not. But I could give you quite a time of it. I could
amuse myself with you as a cat with a mouse. As the Lord with Job.*

You remember what He said to Job: Whatsoever is under the whole heaven is mine. 41:11.

The whole heaven of this fiction, you mean. And what limited manner of Lord is *that*, created by the author of the book? That's a Lord less than the author, less even that *you*."

Precisely. Still want to fuck with me?

"The fact remains: I know who said the above unattributed statement, and you do not. The unnaturally thin woman with no nose and no breasts said it."

(Questions for study: Does the unnaturally thin young woman exist or not? Is she present in this classroom or is she not? Are others present? Or have we only a bearded young man and a professor who is close to the heart of his author? Do we assume that the classroom, being a classroom, is full or nearly full? On what basis do we make that assumption? Or do we not know either way? Does it matter? Has the professor earned our trust as a character? For if he has, we might reasonably assume that he is not lying when he tells us that the exclamation made above was uttered by the unnaturally thin young woman with no nose and no breasts. But is it possible for a character in a fiction to know something the author of the fiction does not know? The character is a spark from the fire of the author's mind: does the spark contain the entire pattern of the fire? If a character comes from the unconscious of the author, could he contain knowledge hidden from the author himself? And by analogy, could a man know something hidden from God? Furthermore, what is to be made of the fact that the unnaturally thin young woman's absence of a nose is different from the absences of noses of other characters, for she has explicitly not been given a nose, whereas other characters have only implicitly not been given noses with a few exceptions, most notably the leper in Flaubert's "The Legend of Saint Julian, the Hospitalier," who is also explicitly noseless, as

is the bureaucrat in Gogol's 'The Nose,' whose nose,
however, is found in a bakery, baked into a bun.)

"Consider," stated the professor, "have you ever heard mention of Raskolnikov having a nose? Hamlet? Jean Valjean? Of..." By God, he thought, I'm drawing a blank. I can't think of even one more famous character. He rubbed his nose agitatedly. It began to swell. He closed his eyes again, peered into the red-black curtain of his eyelids. He still was not certain whether the unnaturally thin young woman still was present, whether she ever *truly* had been present except in his imaginary imagination, whether she was standing there with her empty brassiere drooping around her, the elastic clasps sagging against the bird-like bones of her shoulder blades, whether she intended to remove all of her clothing, whether she intended to perform some sexual act. His nose throbbed, ached, burned. It is painful to have a nose, he thought.

"Consider," the professor stated, "Genesis, 2:7: 'And the Lord God formed man of the dust of the ground, and breathed into his *nostrils* (emphasis the professor's) the breath of life; and man became a living soul.' The lesson is clear: no nose, no soul. Consider that in Egypt when one died the soul was believed to fly out the nose. Thus: no nose, no escape from the flesh. Consider that in Rome, the statues of dead Caesars who ceased to be gods had their noses broken off. *Ergo*: No nose, no godliness, no majesty."

"No snot," muttered the bearded young man by the window, smirking into his knuckles.

The professor glanced at him to silence him with attention. "Consider the great Cathedral of Bern, whose magnificent roof, Jung tells us, was destroyed in the late nineteenth century by an enormous snot dropped from the heavens, thus rendering the Cathedral once again an open receptacle of Grace."

"Shit," said the bearded young man. "Turd. It was turd that done it, a giant turd from the heavens."

"The nose," continued the professor, closing his eyes again and ignoring the outspoken young man, "is important in history."

A very tall young man with a very large young nose seated at the very center of the last row raised his chin and said, "You have a nice nose as noses run. Did you pick it yourself? Let me know when you get to the bridge and we can all cross over." Then he leaped to his feet and in sudden rage shouted, "I'm a Jew. I sneeze green snot!"

"Bunch crapola," muttered the bearded young man. "it's all a great big bunch of overintellectualized crapola."

The professor's eyes still were closed, raising a serious question for study about point-of-view. If, as certain prominent authors and critics assert, a given fiction must hold unswervingly to a single point of view for functional verisimilitude to be maintained, and if, in this specific fiction at hand, the single prevailing point of view is that of the professor, how, given the fact that his eyes were closed, could he know that the statement about sneezing green snot was made by a very tall young man with a very large young nose who had been seated at the very center of the last row? If, on the other hand, as is held by certain other critics and writers, there is no reason why point of view cannot shift as frequently as an author feels it ought, then what are the ramifications of this possible point of view shift? Are we leaving the professor behind now? If not, we might begin to assume that we are working with surreal or superreal or irreal modes here.

In *fact*, the statement made by the young man with the large nose is a statement borrowed from a well-known contemporary fiction and is, in *fact*, a statement made by the fictional Jewish lover of a WASP woman purported to have been modelled upon the wife of a famous American editor who is purported to have served as a model for a main character in the novel. Interestingly, this famous American editor was among the first to publish one of the prime authorities upon which the heart of the nose of this fiction in which we find ourselves at the moment is based.

In *fact*, this famous editor — if, indeed, what you are being told here is not simply more fiction, anti-illusionist illusion...

"Who said that? Who's saying all those paragraphs there? Who?"

Me!

"Who's *me*?"

Me, numbnuts, the guy at the wordprocessor, and may I ask who you are 'cause as far as I can see you are not in this fiction by invitation and your statements are not attributed so kindly get lost or I will subject you to some unpleasant situations. I'm beginning to lose my patience.

"Oh, yeah, well screw you, author! Who do you think you are? God?"

Okay, punk, on your feet.

"You never gave me any! You never gave me anything! All I have is a goddamn fucking voice, you stingy motherfucker!"

Okay, punk, now you got 'em. Feet. Big feet. Much too big for your stubby little legs and fat ass. And ingrown toenails. And bunions. And you there, Beard, come here. I want you to step on this punk's foot. Use your weight.

"Get real, jerk."

Hey, beard. You said that to me? Your author?

"I never asked to be written."

Oh, no, huh? Well, how would you like to be erased? Slowly. How would you like me to rub you out with one of those round, flinty, old-fashioned typewriter erasers and whisked away with one of those blue nylon whiskbrushes, just so many rubber crumbs. I could do it, you know. Print you and erase you, then delete you from the disk. Easy. How would you like me to delete you up to your neck and then write honey all over your face and process up a plague of velvet ants?

"Hey, come on, huh?" the bearded young man whimpered. "What are you picking on me for? I didn't do anything."

(I confess to a certain perverse pleasure at having so thoroughly broken the bullish young man's spirit, although it makes me fonder of him, too, which makes me

98

wish to bolster his ego again. I am not the type to go around indiscriminately slapping people down. Nor would I arbitrarily delete one of my creature's dignity. No. Not this god. I would not create a world in which the only way for the beasts to survive, for example, is by biting each other in the throat and chewing and swallowing. Not me. It's right there in The Book. *Check out Genesis: Quote: And surely your blood of your lives will I require at the hand of every beast and at the hand of man — Unquote. I mean, you talk about your crazy fucked-up types. You talk about your mean Marquises. This God character has got a mighty weird sense of sport, I would say.*)

The professor stood waving his arms at the desk, shouting from the screen of the computer through the rapidfire tapping of the keys: "Hey, you up there! God! Can you stick to the point? I've got a presentation to make here. First of all, could you get rid of the speaking feet? You left them dangling there, and they're starting to, well, stink."

The feet are and shall remain secluded and isolated up above unless you insist on continuing to mention them and carry them forward, smart guy. You create your own stinking agony.

"Okay, then, fine. Next point. You began to introduce an interesting aside concerning point of view, external reference and elements of the *roman à clef* in American fiction and then all of a sudden you're off on a rant about God. I mean the other God, the God of Gods. YWHW. Him Who Am. Author of things. *L'Auteur des choses.* Listen, take my advice: *To this haven-bestowed, this due degree of blindness, submit. The proper study of mankind is man.*"

Well, let me ask you this then, professor. How would you like it if I created those conditions for you to live in? How would you like it if I withheld key information from you, kept you blind? Would you like it? Would you just submit? Would you thank me for it?

The professor closed his eyes again, peered into the red-black darkness. The room was silent. He recalled having seen a window, but realized now that he had forgotten to look and see if there were a door. For if there were no door, it was entirely possible that he was in one of those existential hells which used to be so fashionable in French literature and on *The Twilight Zone*, doomed for all time to stand here behind this desk with an aching nose and uncomfortable throbbing erection pressed against the wooden edge of the desk brought about by the real or imagined image of an unnaturally thin young woman undressing right in the middle of his classroom. Small tits. The professor had a thing for women with small tits, the smaller the better; it was his weakness in life, his *thing*, his *bag*, if you will, and this was the first time in his life he had ever encountered a woman with no tits at all. His erection was furious. On the other hand, perhaps he was dreaming. For in one's dreams, as has been observed from antiquity, he thought, all manner of strange things occur — we even sleep with our mothers, as Socrates observed.

The professor blushed. Why, he wondered, had that thought occurred to him? What, he wondered, was the significance of his attraction to small-breasted women? His own mother had, in fact been quite busty.

It occurred to him then that perhaps his Oedipal fixation was so strong that it sought its disguise in this specialized desire in order to minimize the apparent motherness of womanness, to disguise the Oedipalness of his imagining.

The professor hobbled out from behind the desk, paused, stricken, looked down at his foot. The entire duration of his existence had been spent behind a desk. He did not know until this moment that he had a club foot. Swollen, he thought. Swollen foot. He took a handkerchief from his pocket and patted his forehead. The word *Oedipus*, he knew of course, could etymologically be traced to that meaning, the wound on the baby's feet when carted off by the father's servant for death, and what was the implication of the swollen factor, a swollen foot, a swollen organ?

Am I mad? he thought.

Is God a literalist of the imagination? Or am I a mere fragment in the fantasy of the fool at the wordprocessor?

He peered out over the classroom, blinking, leaning forward incredulously.

All was changed, changed utterly. Everything that had been there before was gone: the bearded young man (gone), the speaking feet (gone), the very tall young man with the very large young nose (gone), the unnaturally thin young woman (gone), the professor's erection (gone), the professor's author (nowhere in sight or hearing). The classroom was now full of people, row after row of them.. *And they were all exactly alike!* (Emphasis mine.) They sat erect in their seats, hands folded before them. They were smiling, but their eyes were hidden by a static glint of light off their spectacles, giving them the appearance of smiling blind men. They were all men, all bald, and none had a nose, no, not one of them, all were noseless.

The room was still.

Slowly, the professor placed the heels of his hands against his temples and, reeling, tilted his face up toward the sky. The room had no ceiling. Up above was blue sky touched here and there with puffs of stylized cumulus.

All movement ceased.

The fiction now becomes a painting: classroom with no ceiling, row after row of identical bald, noseless men, clubfooted professor clutching his skull and gazing upward. The professor's face is seen in inversion, bent back so that the forehead is first in the perspective, lower than the mouth. The perspective is from above. The viewer looks in and down upon the scene, much as God might. Or a bird of prey.

TORTURING YOUR SENTENCES:
The Brutal Art of Self-Editing

There is no happiness like mine.
I have been killing darlings.

In *Joysprick, An Introduction to the Language of James Joyce*, Anthony Burgess defines two classes of writing which he refers to as Class 1 and Class 2. He identifies Class 1 writing as the language of the popular novel in which "language is a zero quantity, transparent, unseductive, the overtones of connotation and ambiguity totally damped." As examples he refers to "the American Irvings...Stone and Wallace"

"Such work," he writes, "is closer to film than to poetry and it invariably films better than it reads. (Its) aim...can only properly be fulfilled when the narrated action is transformed into represented action: content being more important than style, the referents ache to be free of their words and to be presented directly as sense data."

The Class 2 writer, Burgess says, is concerned with the opacity of language — as was James Joyce, most notably in *Ulysses* and *Finnegan's Wake*.

Obviously, there are works where the two types of writing overlap. "Transparent language...can be elevated to a high level of esthetic interest through wit, balance, euphony, and other devices of elegance." And Class 2 language can be carried to an extreme where all but the most elevated reader will begin to tire of it. Even poetry combines the two, even the purest poetry is unlikely to be pure language — as Forster sighs in *Aspects of the Novel*: A story, oh dear, yes, I suppose there must be a story.

What I think of as the best fiction combines the best qualities of both "classes" and does so in the sense that form and content are inextricable. What we say is inherent in how we say it, as John Ciardi pointed out in his book *How Does a Poem Mean?* Or as Wright Morris said, "Change your syntax and you change your mind." *Six hundred cavalrymen rode into a valley in which they were killed.* "Into the valley of death rode the six hundred..." The words Tennyson chose have the rhythm of horseback and give life to the content.

Gladys Swan says, "Vision dictates form." In other words, you will probably not find yourself in a situation where you get a vision, or perhaps you prefer to call it an idea, and then sit down and discuss with yourself what form to give it. Most likely the form will devise itself in the course of the writing or will be present as a seed from the start. The writer's most important job, I think, is to be a receptive vehicle for the expression as it occurs, to know how to sort the genuine from the false in transmitting the song.

In Bernard Malamud's metafiction *Pictures of Fidelman*, he humorously handles the theme of form and content in art when the artist Fidelman, who has dug a series of holes in the earth as an exercise in pure form, is visited by the devil who smacks Fidelman on the head with his shovel, knocking him into one of the holes: "So," the devil says. "Now you got form *and* content." A grave.

Just as we must be open to the initial rush of our words, we must also be willing in a cool mind to edit our manuscripts until the prose is as perfect as we can make it. William Faulkner talked about killing your darlings; we must be willing to listen to those darlings scream and die if and as necessary.

In *On Writing*, Henry Miller gives this interesting piece of advice to writers: "When you can't write, work." I take that to mean that a writer's primary job is to create, to do the actual spade work of the writing, but that when we are not doing the actual writing, there are many other things that have to be done; one of the primary of these secondary jobs is that of editing ourselves. Wordsworth's tranquil recollection of the spontaneous overflow. It is via this process that the writer distinguishes his or her work as a finished, polished, professional piece of art.

Among the acts involved in this process are considerations of a major structural nature, where to drop, cut, add, reshape, etc. But there are also more or less "minor" or "small" matters to consider, small in the sense of ensuring that a piston is free of sand, and that is what I would like to talk about here.

Let's say one day you hear someone say something in a certain way and the sound of that being said reminds you of something you once heard at another time of your life, reminds you of something that happened. The memory continues to move, fuses with something else inside, and suddenly you are hearing sentences spoken in a voice that compels you to begin to write, perhaps first merely by jotting down fragments of scenes, sentences, phrases. The flow increases, like ice melting off a mountain. A trickle becomes a stream. Soon the whole thing is flowing like a river, turning, widening, narrowing, roaring.

And then it's done. You have your story down on paper. You are delighted. It is like being in love. You feel a glow. You are very happy. Next day, you take out the manuscript, read it through again. You are still in love, but you begin to perceive small flaws, little irritations, discontents.

At this point, the difference between love and writing is that if you try to change your lover, you are not likely to succeed. In love, you must learn to live with the flaws. In fiction, you must learn to fix them. And this is why we edit, why editing is so necessary. We have to sit down with the manuscript and run it through again and again and again, doing what Sena Jeter Naslund calls torturing your sentences to make sure they can take it, until you have your product as polished and complete as you are able to make it — so that your prose functions as language, giving body to your vision, rather than as a lens through which the reader peers to see the film that might have been made out of your story.

There are a number of things I am alert to when I am reviewing my own draft stories or the pieces submitted to workshops I teach. Following are the main things I look for in terms of language. I would also like to underscore, however, what seems to me an important point: one ought to be as aware of the possibilities of exception as of rules. Otherwise we risk becoming guilty of what we are sometimes charged with: writing and teaching State Fiction, promoting "sameness."

Excess verbiage — less says more/more says less -- repetitions
It is always advisable when editing a manuscript to keep an eye open for whatever we can cut without loss or, better yet, with benefit. Typically, when we are writing the first draft of a story, we go further than necessary, unnecessarily repeat and emphasize things. Sometimes we go so far as to repeat a word in the primitive belief that saying it twice will make it stronger: "Gently, gently he took her hand." Two times gently is still only gently. Is a black black sky blacker than a black sky? Maybe sometimes, but not usually. Of course, there are exceptions, famous ones. No one could be lonelier than Coleridge's ancient mariner, "Alone, alone, all all alone/Alone on a wide wide sea."

And consider these lines from Eliot's "Prufrock":
    "I am Lazarus
    Come back from the dead
    Come back to tell you all
    I will tell you all."
Would this be better as,
    "I am Lazarus
    Come back from the dead
    To tell you all"?
Clearly not.

And what is one to make of the following bit of prose:

106

"Touch me. Soft eyes. Soft soft soft hand. I am lonely here. O, touch me soon now. What is that word known to all men? I am quiet here alone. Sad too. Touch touch me."

Should we edit that? Who wrote it? Jim Morrison? No, James Joyce — it is from, no, not Leopold or Molly's scenes, but the intellectual Stephen Dedalus as he walks along the beach in the Proteus scene in *Ulysses*.

I do not intend to try to help James Joyce write better — as Cynthia Ozick illustrates so skillfully in her fiction-essay, "Helping T. S. Eliot Write Better," in which she has Eliot fall into the clutches of an influential editor who wants to do a job on "The Love Song of J. Alfred Prufrock." Among other things, he wants Eliot to cut the repetitions, "There will be time, there will be time..." And, "In the room the women come and go/talking of Michelangelo..." *You already said that before - twice!*

Still, most repetitions are dull and most first drafts are full of eminently cuttable verbage.

In the first chapter of this book I mention how effectively a writing-teacher once pointed this out to me. Edward Hoagland at C.C.N.Y., more than 30 years ago, in a personal writing conference, read out to me three sentences I had written. Something like:

> "He pulled his chair up to the desk, then turning
> around, so his back was to the chair, lowered
> himself to the seat. Then he crossed his left leg
> across his right knee."

Hoagland leaned across the desk, clutched and hammered his fist furiously in the air and said, "You are including every fucking detail!"

So even though I will never forget that, I do forget from time to time and have to keep looking with fresh eyes at my mansucripts for the odd word, the odd phrase, the odd sentence, paragraph, that I can lope away with a stroke of the pen, making the prose tighter, neater, more effective.

A good piece of training is to keep your eyes open when you

read other people's work for sentences that you find particularly effective. Often, they will be small sentences that create an enormous effect in your consciousness. You will remember them as large things, but when you go back to the book for another look, you often find them to be small, lean bits.

Here's an example from Andre Dubus's story "Waiting," a description of a woman watching the sea at night:

"Black waves broke with a white slap, then a roar.
She sat huddled in the cool air."

Two little sentences yet they evoke a whole picture of a beach at night, the sea, the sound and feel of it, the color, the woman sitting huddled there, the temperature, a whole scene in seventeen words lucidly evoking three senses.

Here is such a sentence from Dylan Thomas's "The Peaches," of two boys set loose in the country on holiday:

"Down the thick dingle Jack and I ran shouting, scalping the brambles with our thin stick-hatchets."

Or consider Hemingway's opening:

"He was an old man who fished alone in a skiff in the Gulf Stream and he had gone eighty-four days without taking a fish."

Would it be stronger if it were written to give us more information, a more detailed picture, more sensory evocation, like this say?

"He was an elderly man, perhaps sixty-seven, white-haired, brown-eyed, with muscular heavily veined hands, and he had been fishing all by himself in an old battered wooden skiff that had once been painted yellow but was now weathered and grey, in the choppy blue waters of the Gulf Stream where for more than two months he had not caught even one fish, not even a sardine."

On the other hand, I wouldn't like to come off as a champion of minimalism, or as the old *New Yorker* philosophy was once characterized: *No vivid writing, please!* (The New *New Yorker*, of course, is something quite else.) Just think of some of the fine lavish sentences of Norman Mailer or John Updike or John Barth — "Among the fools and fops of seventeenth century London, there ranged one awkward, gangling fetch known as Ebenezer Cooke." (Opening sentence of *The Sotweed Factor*.)

And a lot of people would like to do a job on Thomas Wolfe, but who would *really* wish to reduce this:

> "O lost, and by the wind grieved, ghost, come back again." Or "We seek the great forgotten language, the lost land-end into heaven, a stone, a leaf, an unfound door."

Think, too, of Dylan Thomas's "Child's Christmas in Wales":

> "All the Christmases roll down toward the two-tongued sea like a cold and headlong moon bundling down the sky that was our street. And I stop at the rim of the ice-edged fish-freezing waves and plunge my hand into the snow and bring out whatever I can find. In goes my hand into that wool-white bell-tongued ball of holidays resting at the rim of the carol-singing sea and out comes..." etc.

It would be a crime of grievous proportions to workshop down the likes of that. Or what about this famous conclusion to a wonderful story:

> "Oh what can you do with a man like that? What can you do? How can you dissuade his eye in a crowd from seeking out the cheek with acne, the infirm hand; how can you teach him to respond to the inestimable greatness of the race, the harsh surface beauty of life, how can you put his finger for him on the obdurate truths before which fear and horror are powerless? The sea that morning was iridescent and dark. My wife and my sister

were swimming...and I saw their uncovered heads, black and gold in the dark water. I saw them come out, and I saw that they were naked, unshy, beautiful and full of grace, and I watched the naked women walk out of the sea."

Cheever did not often get that lavish but I think he did memorably on that conclusion to "Goodbye, My Brother," which, it is said, he composed and recited in full voice, fortified by several gins, while walking with his family out of a New York restaurant one evening.

And what minimalist even is likely to come up with something like this from Eliot's *Waste Land?*

"A current under sea picked his bones in whispers."

Or Joyce's,

"Father hunted the children out of the field with a blackthorn stick."

When we edit ourselves, we often must cut and reduce, but neither does it hurt to have the music of the poets in our hearts and ears. Fiction needs such sentences.

Another kind of excess verbiage is found in repetition of words within a sentence or in close proximity and repetition of information. If you tell us in one paragraph that a man is wearing a red hat, we remember that. You don't have to remind the reader of such things. You shouldn't, in fact. It is annoying. Also it can be awkward to repeat words within a sentence. *But he didn't want to hurt her, though.* Or, *Abruptly he uttered a sudden shout.* Or, *She had remembered that he had told her about all the things they had done that summer, hadn't she?* (See also pluperfect, under Verbs below).

It sometimes helps to read your sentences aloud. Andre Dubus II once told me when he thought he was finished with a story, he would read it aloud into a tape recorder and play it back and then go on to the final revisions.

Prose Texture and Stage Directions

One of the lessons I had as a writer which stuck to me came from Alex Blackburn, editor of *Writers' Forum*, who encouraged me for a few years there with constuctive critical rejections (before finally accepting several pieces). On one occasion he returned only one page of one of my stories to me, and he had drawn a circle around one of the sentences — "She walked across the room." — and wrote in the margin, "This kind of sentence pulls no weight." This made me aware of a tendency in my prose to write what I came to think of then as "stage directions": *He walked across the room. He opened the door and went in. He turned around. He climbed the stairs.*

There is nothing wrong with these sentences per se and they might be used in fictions, but they can also be lethal, dead wood verbiage that pulls, as Alex Blackburn indicated, no fictional weight. There is no room in a short fiction for a sentence that is not pulling its weight. In a play script where it says, "He picks up a book," or whatever, an actor is waiting to give flesh, blood, and movement to it. Picture Marlon Brando carrying out a stage direction like: *He crosses the room.* Or Robert De Niro, Bette Davis, Lauren Bacall, Madonna. Picture your own character doing it.

Joyce, in *Ulysses,* has many scenes of people walking. How does *he* do it? Here's Leopold Bloom: *His slow feet walked him riverward.* Here's Stephen Dedalus: *Stephen closed his eyes to hear his boots crush crackling wrack and shells.* (Talk about your onomatopoeia.) Here's another example, from a workshop piece manuscript describing a fellow fleeing in the middle of the night from an unhappy love: *The floorboards moaned beneath his feet.* (Joseph Curtin, "Doors.")

Or, again, from Dylan Thomas's "The Peaches": "I climbed the stairs; each step had a different voice."

Or Joyce, in *Giacomo Joyce*: "High heels clack hollow on the resonant stone stairs."

After sentences like that, it is difficult to allow one's

character to simply walk across the room.

Again, while such sentences may sometimes be useful and necessary and perfectly valid, in general a proliferation of them make for a weakly moving fiction, one that trudges stolidly and linearly along and causes the reader's attention to nod, causes the reader to begin to scan rather than read, as Flannery O'Connor cautions in her wonderful *Mystery and Manners*.

One can try to take divergent angles of narration and description. Think of yourself as a movie camera going for angle play, try to visualize things other than straight head on linear. Instead of showing only the faces of characters who sit straight up in straight back chairs and converse point for point, talking heads, try and look under the table at their feet, their hands on their knees, their fingers playing nervously at a coffee mug, the scuff on the toe of a shoe, a pimple at the corner of the nose that keeps attracting the fingers. Consider matters from different directions, a view of faces, furniture, feet, sky, through the eyes of a cat. Leap! Twist! Move!

Also you can avoid stage-direction-like sentences by just dropping them. Some writer once said he quit or ran into a life-long block because it was so much trouble getting his characters from one room to another. But in fact you don't have to. Unlike human beings, characters do not have corporeal existences. As William H. Gass pointed out in his *Fiction and the Figures of Life*, any number of characters go through their stories without, so far as he knew, ever having eaten anything or even having the organs necessary to the other vital functions. They make love without our ever having been told they possess the necessary instruments to do so.

The writer is free to select only those details and actions which further his story, only the telling details, and drop all the rest. How do you get a character from one room to another? You employ a full stop, change paragraph, and there he or she is, elsewhere, right where you want them to be.

She looked at the kitchen sink, heaped with

gravey-slimed plates and utensils. (New paragraph): In the bedroom she folded back the covers and crawled in between the crisp white sheets.

A final word on movement of characters: Alec Guinness who had a genius for portraying character in his films would plan his method by watching the movement of animals in the zoo and people walking on the streets. One of the ways he got to the point of understanding a character was by first determining how the character walks. A dimension of character surely of use to a fiction writer as well.

Linearity and Ideas

Closely related to this is the topic of linearity and ideas. Trying to let things run in logical sequence and to embody logical ideas can be lethal to a fiction. Some writers, especially Europeans, do it well. Camus managed to do it very successfully, although some complain his work reads like a philosophy text. His *Caligula* is an amazing dramatic representation of ideas. Dostoevski, too, excels at this, although the fusion of idea, character, and event in his work is so seamless that it is difficult to imagine it occurring other than spontaneously. Thomas Mann, of course, is another — his masterful portrait of the ascendant fascist in "Mario and the Magician," for example. Still, I believe that most fiction, while it can be mined for ideas, is not *built* of them. Stendahl, talking about one of his books, said that it was full of ideas, but not one of them was his.

Mann's Cavaliere Cipolla in "Mario and the Magician" is first of all a clearly drawn character, a creature of the imagination so real that he touches a deep, resonant chord in the soul; that his existence also has political, sociological, societal implications is dependent upon the clarity and credibility of his creation — were he less a character, he would be mere propaganda, like the ordinary old Chinese worker invented to speak the party line on Tiananmen Square.

113

I believe that a fiction writer doesn't think in ideas so much as in fictional elements. Things go together the way the human body goes together: Here there are arms, there a nose, and the road turns here the way it turns because you can *see* it turn that way or at least you can *feel* it does. I would caution writing students against *thinking* too much, or trying to *think* their way forward in a fiction. Rather *imagine* your way forward. Think with your whole being, but not with logical or moral expectation. Who was it said the fiction writer's job is to sit and wait to catch the policemen of his mind asleep? Beware the linear. Go roaming. *Imagine.* Think of Gordon Weaver's Vietnam tunnel rat in "Under the World" *imagining* his way forward through the darkness of the enemy's underground tunnels. Or inversely, think of the confused coach in Weaver's "Hog's Heart," who tries to fire up his football team to go out and tear the other team into shreds by shouting, "I want to see some *thinking* out there today, boys!" And again think of John Updike's comparison of writing to driving at night: You can't see beyond the beams of your headlights, but if you keep following them you will get there.

And while there is a convention to avoid abrupt transitions in fiction, there is much to be said for creative disruption. One of the most memorable sentences I have ever come across flashed almost subliminally into a piece of writing by William H. Gass in *The Habitations of the Word* — in the midst of a lengthy rhetero-philosophical consideration this sentence suddenly appears: *What good has liking olives ever done me?*

The lesson from that is: True, avoid confusedly jolting transitions, but do not fear stunningly abrupt departures.

Riding home on the subway once on a hot summer New York City day, I stood nodding by the doors on the F train rattling beneath the East River. My eyes sleepily slipped across the face of a woman standing on the other side of the car, whereupon without prelude or warning, she dropped into a crouch and shouted, "I don't know who you are! Or who you think you are! But you don't know me. So keep your eyes to yourself!" I was

114

startled, frightened even, but I shall never forget that woman or the beautiful gift she gave me: a brilliant, passionate bouquet of little sentences, and a lesson in the skillful use of abrupt transition.

While a fiction is bound, Forster supposes in *Aspects of the Novel*, to have a story, and a story is bound, I suppose, to have a beginning, middle and end, it is not bound to move in a single straight line from one end to the other. One of the great lessons on human existence which we had from Joyce on the simultaneity of time in our consciousness makes it difficult to think in the thin lines of a single tense. The present is only a deepening of the past melting into the future. Fiction which tries to ignore that fact, or to ignore the fact that life is one great unanswered question composed of a myriad of other mostly unanswered smaller ones will be fiction that is wooden, shallow, and unreal.

The mind has wings and can make enormous leaps and so can fiction; the only rule is that it not jar the reader — at least not ineffectively so.

Another thing not to fear is the way things seem to just come together sometimes. It was a great revelation for me as a writer the way anything that happens to you while you're writing something is liable to become a part of what you're writing — perhaps because when you are charged, the electricity of it touches and transforms all manner of detail and turns it into a part of the work.

There's a fine example of that in a story by Francois Camoin, "Diehl: The Wandering Years." It is about a writer who becomes blocked when his main character buries himself beneath the front lawn of his house with nothing but a tube up to the surface for air and communication. His wife comes out that first night and speaks down the tube to him: *How can you do this to me?* she asks. Then she begins to stuff dirt down the pipe. The writer gets blocked, leaves his real-life-fictional wife and drives to California to visit his old writing teacher who, he learns, is dying of cancer. The teacher and the wife welcome him to stay and work on his novel there, but to his dismay he finds himself falling in love with his teacher's wife. Diehl sits in his work room typing away at his novel, and his main character is back under the front lawn, and the wife is whispering invective down the pipe to him, until suddenly his teacher's wife comes in and whispers to Diehl's back, "I love you." *I love you*, Diehl types, and it becomes what his character's wife is saying to his character down the pipe. "Please don't be dead," she says. "I'm sorry. I'm sorry. Please."

There is an old textbook titled *Understanding Fiction*, edited by Cleanth Brooks and Robert Penn Warren within which there is a section called "Fiction and Human Experience: How Four Stories Came to Be Written." The section contains four stories and a statement by the author of each about the writing of the story in question. One of the stories is Cheever's "Goodbye, My Brother," and he tells how there are a number of elements in it that came from life and were greatly separated from one another in time, place, and context, but what that confirmed for him, that they all came together eventually into a single story, was the greater continuity of life, of the underlying meaning of life, stretching beyond gaps to form a fictional whole. (I speak more about this in other chapters of this book.)

Verbs

Another point which requires close attention when we self-edit is the choice of verbs. The verb is the muscle of a sentence and while you don't want your sentences muscle-bound and stiff or bulging like a body builder, a fiction does require strong, lean, active sentences, lithe as a river or a cat. *He walked down the street. He picked up the book. She removed the cellophane from the package. He went down the alley. He ate the apple.* It's not just the verbs that are weak, the whole approach is. Turn it around. Not, *We crossed the field.* But, "We set off across the field along the footpath she and her friends had beaten to and from her place. Before me, tilting as she limped, her full black skirt swayed about her calves." (Meredith Steinback, "In Recent History.") Not, *He looked into*

116

her eyes. But, "Howie was peering into her eyes with an expression of concern..." ("The Ape Lady in Retirement," T. Coraghessan Boyle.) Not, *He walks down the tracks toward the city, holding his gun.* But, "He hurries down the tracks toward the city, gun across his shoulder." (Peter Matthiessen, "Lumumba Lives.")

Joyce again: "A patched white sheet shrouded the piano." Or, "The wings of her drooping hat shadow her false smile."

Onomatopoeic verbs are fine, if not overdone -- sizzle, slash, ring, buzz, swish, bop are certainly better than comic book sound syllables — *bap! bam! wham!* — although Tom Wolfe did well with them.

Another thing to be aware of is *the overuse of expletives with to be.* Sometimes of course this is quite appropriate. Who would argue with, *There was an old lady who lived in a shoe?* Or the opening to Gordon Weaver's "The Interpreter" also referred to earlier:

> "It is as if... It is as if I cannot remember the things I must say to myself. It is as if all the words I know, both in English and Mandarin, have fled from me..."

Obviously a skillful use of expletives and to be, but they are generally overused, especially by would-be minimalists:

> *It was a lousy day. It was the first time he had ever stayed out all night. There wasn't anything he could do to undo that. There wasn't anything he could do at all. What was even worse, there was a visitor there in his house who was sitting there talking to his wife. It was lousy.*

You find it in the best of fictions, too: "What was strange was that there should be a man there at all." This from no less a poet than Robert Penn Warren in his wonderful story, "Blackberry Winter."

It is, it was, there is, there was... There was a lady there who told fortunes. Nothing intrinsically wrong with it, but you have to listen and think about how it sounds, how it flows. A lot of this is a question of ear and taste, but less experienced writers can tend to make the mistake of stringing together a lot of sentences that run on nothing stronger than expletives and *was*, often in weak imitation of writers like Hemingway and Carver, and the result is liable to be a rubble of flaccid sentences, a pool of flesh, like a deboned chicken. Something to think of when self-editing. And study the masters for inspiration — how about a sentence like Joyce's description of a beach: "These heavy sands are language tide and wind have silted here." You won't get that from your dirty realists.

Another problem with verbs is the overuse of *progressive tense: He was sitting on a chair drinking a whiskey.* He sat on a chair drinking a whiskey. Or He sat, drank. I think people sometimes fear that the simple past conveys only an initial motion — he sat (and that was that) — while progressive conveys a motion already initiated and still in progress. But the simple past can also convey a sense of continuing action without clogging up the page with a lot of *ing*'s.

Passive voice is another verb item to we wary of. *The book was given to her by Jim* has its grammatical function, but is almost always weaker than *Jim gave her the book.* No need to deny ourselves the possibility of passive voice, but use it only with consideration. Think about how it sounds, how it functions. *His face was smacked by her* doesn't sound as right as *She smacked his face* although *he got his face smacked* is something else again.

From time to time in workshop manuscripts I also see awkward use of the *pluperfect*. The pluperfect is useful in a fiction running on simple past tense to signal a move into a time preceding the tense of the narration. The pluperfect signals you in, then you switch to simple past again and back to pluperfect to signal out again:

> *He walked down the street and thought about what she had told him. She sat in the kitchen and said it right to his face. She didn't love him anymore. She didn't even like him. In fact, the sight of him made*

her want to puke. He offered her a bucket and took
his leave. Now, out on the street, he was not certain
he had done the right thing.

In fact, pluperfect, like conditional, is rarely needed: *In those days he would walk along the beach, he would toss crumbs of his bagel to the seagulls, he would watch the gulls swoop and cry out, he would wish that she were there.* All those would's are dead wood. You can drop em. *In those days he walked along the beach, tossed crumbs of his bagel to the seagulls, watched them swoop and cry out, wishing she were there.*

Grammar

Which brings to mind another matter worth consideration: grammar. Granted, fiction is not an academic text, but still it might seem reasonable for a fiction writer to be conversant with the principles of grammar of the English language, to own a book or two on grammar, a book on usage, and to consult them from time to time, to refresh the memory of why we construct sentences as we do. Certainly, we are free to break all the rules of grammar we wish for effect, but hopefully we know we are doing so. It gives one a sense of security to know what a dangling participle is, for example, and not to find oneself passing on sentences like, "Reading the sentences, the story escaped me."

Le mot juste

Flaubert's phrase, is a good one to keep in mind: The exact word. If we are describing precise things, there are exact words to use. It does not do for a fiction writer to just dash off a sentence and let it fly without worrying whether the words really convey what he meant them to. Sometimes, of course, they may convey *more*, sometimes our unconscious improves on a weak conscious intention and that is excellent, that is grace, but that is also another matter than what I am dealing with here — that of choosing the exact word; this is the recollection in tranquillity of the spontaneous overflow, and it is here we examine our words, poke and pinch them, to see if they do what we want of them.

You see it all the time in workshop manuscripts. *He removed the wrapping from the motel glass.* How about *tore? The water hit against the pilings.* How about *slapped? The mosquito buzzed at his ear. Whined?* But you don't want to get too fancy — not, *The mosquito violined at his ear.*

Splendid examples of the successful selection of the exact word can be found in most good poems. Here's a sentence from a letter written by Flaubert in 1852: "A really good sentence in prose should be like a good line in poetry, something you cannot change, and just as rhythmic and sonorous." Read the poets.

Sentence rhythm

It is necessary to vary sentence rhythms. Language has its natural rhythms. Narrative and dramatic writing needs variety and ideally that variety should reflect the rhythms and movement of the actions being depicted or at least of appropriate speech patterns or of the voice of the piece in question. Or the psychological balance, or imbalance, of the character or persona whose mental/emotional state the words reflect.

In editing our prose, we must look for places where sentence structures are repeated one after the other and vary them. Where we find a number of compound sentences in a row, we can vary them with a single short one, using the variety at just the point where a variety might seem appropriate.

For example: *It was snowing. It was always snowing at Christmas. December in my memory was white as Lapland, though there were no reindeer. But there were cats.* That is a good example from Dylan Thomas.

Here is a bad one from no one: *I walk up to the house. I knock on the door. He opens the door. I come into the room. We sit at the table. He pours me a drink. I drink the drink. He caps the bottle. He puts it away. He asks what I want. Just to say hello. Hello, he says.*

Where you have single clause declarative sentence after

sentence, vary them with compounds, the occasional triple compound, etc. Where you have sentences starting over and over with personal pronouns and verbs, try turning them around, start with a prepositional phrase: *Into the valley of death rode the six hundred...* On the other hand, I would caution against getting too technical about this or one might end up with a number of variations which will read by the numbers, like some kind of prose mambo.

Sensory detail

Thomas Aquinas wrote that there are five ways to know God, through the senses, and Flannery O'Connor, in *Mystery and Manners* wrote that fiction, like all human communication, comes via the senses. Or perhaps the shadows of the senses. We do not actually smell the air of a fictional seaside, but we are made aware of its existence by being reminded of what a seaside smells like. Sensory evocation is essential to all effective fiction. The ineluctable modality of the visible, audible, etc.

You'll find it in every strong, memorable fiction — from the lice on the wings of an angel in Garcia Marquez, to the leaves of an aspen *ticking* against the windowglass in Carver, to the men in *sulphur-colored pants* in a Eudora Welty story, to you name it... For more on this, see the chapter on "Realism & Other Illusions."

Similes -- are they, like, really necessary?

A good simile or metaphor is powerful because by comparing two unlike things it brings us to a better understanding of both. Certainly this works well with metaphors: "The force that through the green fuse drives the flower drives my green age..." But have you ever noticed that almost the only good similes you run into seem to be self-conscious, ironic ones? In my opinion, it doesn't work very well to say something like, "The calf bleated like a sad child." Or, "The child wept like a bleating calf." Similes are mostly ironic now and perhaps with good reason.

Here in my opinion are some examples of well-functioning

similes:

"They sat on the railing looking out across the merciless sunbaked alley toward the Pacific Ocean shimmering *like a blue-green afterlife* beyond the used car lots." Or: "Her pain hung around her *like an old black bathrobe.* (Both examples from Garrison Keillor.) And who would object to "Float like a butterfly, sting like a bee"?

Ken Kesey uses a lot of similes in *One Flew Over the Cuckoo's Nest* and many of them are quite effective in establishing the mental state of the narrator — for example when he compares the glittering eyes of the hospital attendants with the glitter of tubes in the back of a radio. But when he tells us that the laugh of one character sounded like a rusty nail being pried out of old wood, I wonder if he is not manipulating the reader a bit.

And when the great Sean O'Faolain tells me that the lights in the windows of the Irish country cottages flew past the train "like sparks blown from a central fire," I *know* I am being manipulated and I don't like it. Frank O'Connor also stumbles in this direction with similes of the same nature. And that is often the problem with similes — they have a tendency, like adverbs, to be editorial in nature. And so often they are really not needed, can be cut away without loss, with gain.

Adverbs

Voltaire said that the adjective is the enemy of the noun and the adverb is the enemy of the verb. Adverbs are a perfectly valid part of speech, of course, but they do tend to have an editorial quality and should be used sparingly in fiction. When overused, they make it seem the writer is telling the reader what to feel about something without any "evidence." This is a case of tell over show, and often the adverb is unnecessarily telling what the verb or the situation has already shown:

> *He said tenderly, "Hello, sweet Wilma." Wilma lowered her eyes modestly. He gently gently touched her arm with a feather. She smiled invitingly. He*

hesitated uncertainly averting his eyes. "Is something wrong?" she asked concernedly. He shook his head hopelessly.

Show and tell

Someone once said, "Show don't tell," as a kind of fictional fiat. But if you try to write fiction without ever telling anything, only showing everything, you will quickly find yourself in a narrow, stuffy room playing a kind of pointless game of charades, aching to be allowed to say something straight out for once and just get on with it. After all, do we show a story or do we tell it?

Most good fiction is a mix of show and tell. Narrative sections narrow down to bits of dialogue, dramatic scene, flow outward into narrative again:

> *Throughout those months of winter, Martin and Victoria got into the habit of taking a little wine with their evening meal — at first just a glass, then a whole bottle between them. One evening, as they sat at the table, empty plates still before them, Martin refilled his glass and when he placed the bottle down again, Victoria saw in the light of the candle that it was empty. "Did you get enough wine?" she asked. She watched him. He had the glass to his mouth, drank deeply. "Sorry," he said, then, setting it down again carefully. It was empty. "Did you want more? I'll open another bottle." She saw at once this had been his plan, saw the tension in his gaze. She shook her head and rose to clear away the dishes. After that, she took only water with her meals, and Martin, who continued to open a new bottle each night, grew increasingly defensive and irritable.*

But exposition, narrative must also be sensuous and clear, must have its own rhythms and drama which give it the blood of life.

Finally, as Wayne C. Booth points out in *The Rhetoric of*

Fiction, "Everything (the author) *shows* will serve to *tell*; the line between showing and telling is always to some degree an arbitrary one."

Tin dialogue

Tin dialogue, of course, is a terrible flaw in a fiction. When your fictional characters speak they must convey a sense of human speech — an illusion of human speech even though it is or can be very different from the actual speech you hear in the world. Andy Warhol's so-called novel, *a*, is a good illustration — the print-out of a tape recording of a group of people speaking together for hours, verbatim, with every repetition and stutter included, and it is insufferably boring, not dialogue at all, because dialogue is a distillation of speech. If a person uses a lot of four-letter words, a soldier, say, he might say 'fuck' ten times in two or three sentences, but to convey that idea in fiction you only have to say it once and the reader hears it loudly.

Still, effective dialogue is close to everyday speech, so remember to listen to how the people around you speak, jot it down, take notes, note the ellipsis for effect: E.g.: Not, "Would you care to repeat that?" but "Care to repeat that?" And also look carefully at the dialogue you read in other people's fiction and note how it affects you — when it seems wooden, when it makes you feel, as someone said of George V. Higgins' dialogue, as though you can feel the spray of saliva off the page.

Of course, there are also times when stiff, wooden, or foreign-sounding dialogue is called for to give a sense of otherness to a piece — I was at a workshop a short while back where one of the students was writing a piece set in Russia, and the dialogue read like the Constance Garnett translation of a Doestoevski novel — which was a good strategy. What could be worse than reading what is supposed to be the speech of Russians who are impeccable in their use of 1950s American slang.

Nothing will put the reader to sleep like bad dialogue. My father was fond of scornfully quoting a clinker from a 1940s clashof-British-kingdoms epic: "Come, men, we must storm the citadel!"

In bed one night I watched a few minutes of the film *Ice Station Zebra* on TV and started jotting down dialogue it was so remarkable. It was a scene between Rock Hudson and Lloyd Nolan:

> -Come in, Jamie.
> -Thank you, sir.
> -Sit down, have a chair.
> -Thank you, sir.
> -Drink?
> -Why yes, thank you, sir.
> -I'm a bourbon man myself, but when in Scotland...
> -The mists of Scottish moors, sir.
> -Right. Well, then. Cheers.
> -Cheers, sir.
> (They drink.)
> -Jim. Just what do you know about Ice Station Zebra.
> -Ice Station Zebra, sir? Well, only what I've read in the papers, sir. That there's an ice station...zebra.

And I was unable to record more for the pencil slipped from my fingers as I snorked off into sleep. The above dialogue might be useful if one were portraying a conversational exchange between two persons whose souls had been snatched by small gray men — it is, in fact, almost frighteningly dull — but watch out. Make sure you can hear what your characters say, make sure it rings in your ear, make sure it pulls fictional weight, is not merely conveying information, would diminish rather than improve the fiction if deleted.

I would also caution against seeking inspiration for dialogue from films where actors often combine gutturals with extended method exercises of face and posture. Fictional dialogue is generally something quite other than film dialogue.

125

Voice

Gordon Weaver, who has published many books of fiction and taught writing for over thirty years, tells his creative writing students that voice is everything in writing a fiction. It is the "sound" of the fiction, and once you have that, the fiction flows, and until you have it, nothing much really happens.

This is perhaps part of what Edgar Allan Poe called "the singleness of effect" of the short prose narrative. Voice is elusive to define, probably the auditory or syntactical incorporation of vision, but it is not difficult to identify when we hear it. It has to do with tone, vision and persona. The persona of the narrative voice — and voice has a persona even if it is an objective third person voice. The best advice I've heard about this is to listen for the sound of the voice of what you are writing and be guided by it, follow it. What you begin seriously may start to assume an ironic tone; what you begin comically may turn deadly serious: listen to those turns.

Nor am I talking here about the old idea of "finding your voice." A good writer may have a single voice to some extent — we all recognize Poe or a certain style like Malamud or Philip Roth or Russel Edson — but more likely a good writer has many voices, a voice for every story, because the voice is as inseparable from the story as the vision. It is the persona of the story, the mask the writer lifts before his or her face to tell the story.

Further, voice, narrative persona, and viewpoint are closely and complexly related. I will attempt to touch further on this in the chapter dealing with viewpoint following this one. However, I would refer readers interested in this topic, and who are not familiar with the work, to Wayne C. Booth's *The Rhetoric of Fiction* for a definitive discussion of it. An illuminating summary is also found in Jack Myers and Michael Simms's excellent *Longman Dictionary and Handbook of Poetry*.

Tuning your ear

I find it hard to imagine a good writer who is not a good reader. This does not necessarily mean reading everything — although the more the better — but rather reading deeply and well, at least some of the time. That is surely the best way to tune your ear, to taste the sentences you read, see if you agree with them, focus on the sentences that grab you and try to figure out how and why they do and to bring this fully developed sense with you into the editing of your own fiction. When editing, if you are suddenly in doubt about whether what you have written has the resonance of life in its language, pause and go to your bookshelves, take down a book by someone whose work you admire, or by someone you have never read, crack open a literary journal and start sampling sentences to refresh your sense of what is good and what is not and bring that refreshed sense back to your manuscript with you. A writer cannot afford to be a passive member of the audience; we have to study what is happening to us when we read.

I also find it hard to imagine a good fiction writer who does not regularly read poetry — bearing in mind Flaubert's statement about the similarity between a good line of prose and a good line of poetry. Of course some poetic devices such as phyming would rarely be appropriate to prose. But reading poetry heightens and hones one's sense of language. Personally I find the rhythms of certain poets and poems running through me like my own blood; without them I would feel half empty. Lines from Joyce, Eliot, Dylan Thomas, Neruda, Rilke, Stafford, Frost, Jack Myers, Roethke, Shakespeare, Chaucer, Arnold, Wordsworth, Sappho...

"April is the cruellest month, breeding
     lilacs out of the dead land, mixing memory
     and desire, stirring dull roots with spring rain..."
(And the original it refers to at the opening of *The Canterbury Tales*.)

"What are these roots that clutch, what
     branches grow out of this stony rubbish?"

"The brief sun flames the ice on pond and/ditches."

"Here I am, an old man in a dry month
Being read to by a boy, waiting for rain."

Consider how Dylan Thomas could ignite a sentence like a
string of little surprises so you can hardly catch your breath:
"The force that through the green fuse drives the flower
Drives my green age; that blasts the roots of trees
Is my destroyer...
And I am dumb to tell the crooked rose
My youth is bent by the same wintry fever..."
Or:
"Light breaks where no sun shines;
where no sea runs, the waters of the heart
Push in their tides;
And broken ghosts with glow-worms in their heads
The things of light
File through where no flesh decks the bones...
A candle in the thighs/warms youth."
Or:
"It is a winter's tale
That the snow blind twilight ferries over/the lakes."

And what fiction writer would not be proud to have written
Mathew Arnold's setting of this scene:
"The sea is calm tonight.
The tide is full, the moon lies fair
Upon the straits -- on the French coast the light
Gleams and is gone; the cliffs of England stand,
Glimmering and vast, out in the tranquil bay.
Come to the window, sweet is the night air!"

We need sentences like that in our fiction. Whether our aim

is to write Class 1 or Class 2 fiction, whether we write like lottery players, hoping for the jackpot or, as Dylan Thomas claimed to exercise his craft or sullen art

"for the lovers, their arms
Round the griefs of the ages,
Who pay no praise or wages..."

ILLICIT ENTRIES INTO PRIVATE MINDS:
On Point of View Shift in Fiction

"Reality is but a point of view."
  -Paul Klee

Just over a hundred years ago, when Robert Louis Stevenson shifted first person points of view from Jim Hawkins to Doctor Livesey in Chapter 16 of *Treasure Island* and back again in Chapter 19, he solved the technical problem of potential reader confusion by hanging signs over the changes: "Narrative Continued by the Doctor" and "Narrative Resumed by Jim Hawkins." A straightforward solution just naive enough to work. In those days, few readers were likely to bristle over authorial intrusion or to worry about the aesthetic/existential implications of an asymmetrical point of view shift. And Stevenson *was* writing for *Young Folks*.

Still, his points of view are tight as a drum; what we know we know through Jim, even if we have to fall into the apple barrel with him for the knowledge. And when we shift to Livesey, Jim is gone and remains unaware of what the reader learns in his absence. There is no all-knowing presence to present overview to the reader, no broth of narrative omniscience, no reader's throne to the right of God's.

Probably anyone who has taken a formal course in writing or has read a book on the topic will know that some narrative theorists and more than a few writing teachers consider point of view shift potentially lethal to a fiction's integrity — particularly in the case of the compact kind of fiction that has appeared over the past 150 years or so, heralded by Poe's theories and Hawthorne's practice. Poe spoke — in a review of Hawthorne's *Twice Told Tales* in 1842 — of the "singleness of effect" of the short prose narrative, which leads to a "sense of the fullest satisfaction...in the mind of him who contemplates it with a kindred art."

Surely, this refinement of technique and the reader's kindred art are related to the gradual displacement of the author-omniscient point of view which, for want of any alternative, had previously prevailed. Wayne C. Booth, in *The Rhetoric of Fiction*, speaks of Boccaccio's habit of shifting point of view "with a total disregard for the kind of technical focus or consistency generally admired today." Booth suggests that we are troubled by point of view shift because it reminds us of the author's presence, noting that there can be no illusion of life when there is no bewilderment, and the omniscient narrator is obviously not bewildered for he has x-ray vision. Yet, he asks, if we are to object, say, to Flaubert's point of view quick shifts from one mind to another in *Madame Bovary*, why not object to *all* inside views as Forster did?

Curiously, Flaubert begins *Bovary* from a first person plural point of view which gradually gives way to a variety of third persons, a technique which can also be seen in Thomas Mann. An interesting, if risky, venture, I would think, for an author to create a persona purporting to speak for an entire community or group.

In *The Art of Fiction*, John Gardner suggests that the growing doubt of the existence of God or objective truth was accompanied by mistrust of the author-omniscient technique and inspired point of view innovation by writers like Dickens, Conrad, James, and Crane, who invented alternatives to omniscience by employing various points of view, a series of unreliable narrators.

There are, of course, different ways to shift point of view. The amateur shifts recklessly, unknowingly, like an intoxicated driver, drifting into another lane and jerking back again seeming not to know quite what happened. A wild genius like Dostoevski does it boldly and to great advantage, Mailer with cunning structural symmetry in *The Naked and the Dead*, although like Stevenson, he too hung a sign over such shifts of time and focus — he called it "The Time Machine" and added names to it as well as he detoured from the onward movement of his novel to explore the past histories of the various characters. In *Land Where My Fathers Died*, Andre Dubus hangs names over each shift, as Faulkner did in *As I Lay Dying*, indicating by the name whose eyes, mind, or stream of experience the coming section is to be viewed from. Harold Robbins — good at structure if nothing else — uses point of view shift to lace up all his tension and suspense, while John Gardner, in *Nickel Mountain*, did it with an uncharacteristic disregard for symmetry, and Andre Dubus in *Voices from the Moon*, did it to achieve balance and range in his short novel about human beings seeking one another, as well as to accomplish the vision promised by the title. Gordon Weaver, otherwise a stickler for the single point of view theory, uses the shift to great advantage in his triptych novel *Circling Byzantium* in which the three points of view constitute a fictional experience of time's three stages — subject, theme, and form welded seamlessly, while his most recent novel, *The Eight Corners of the World*, maintains a single point of view for over 400 pages in the form of the pidgin slang monologue of the book's main character, Yamaguchi.

Most postmodernists would not be caught dead worrying about such trivial technicalities, one of the quintessential aspects of that religion being, perhaps, the bold sin against conventions of the past. Coover, Hawkes, Crews, Pynchon, make it their business to breach traditions, lines, time zones, whatever. Interestingly, though, amidst all the experiments of John Barth's *Lost in the Funhouse*, there is an overriding loyalty to the single point of view, while even a realist like Andre Dubus shifted as he pleased: in his very short novella, "Separate Flight," he made a single brief shift from Beth to Peggy; in "The Pretty Girl," he shifted from a first person Ray to a third person Polly back to a first person Ray and ends, after Ray's death, with a first person Alex.

Perhaps the essence of it is akin to the magician's loyalty to the secrets of his illusions. A human being seems to have but one point of view, into which he or she is locked for the duration. We are not gods. We cannot see into the hearts of others. Or can we? Well, the problem is that if and when we do bridge that gap of separation, we always have to make allowance for the possibility of that leap being a product of paranoia. If we are to maintain the mask of sanity in human society, we do not go about telling people, "I can *see* what you are thinking!" Similarly, many writers feel that to maintain an even keel of illusion in a fiction, a single point of view is essential, a unity of standpoint. Why? Well, the powers of point of view integrity which can be observed in fictions as distant in time from one another as Hawthorne's "My Kinsmen, Major Molineux," Cather's "Paul's Case," and Salinger's *Catcher in the Rye*, all dealing with similar themes and situations, make a good case for the prejudice against the shift.

Yet, still, what we are talking about here is illusion. For if one writer can do three so vastly different points of view, say, as Alexander Portnoy and *Goodbye Columbus's* Neil or the hero of the Zuckerman trilogy, why not the three points of view in one fiction? Gladys Swan, who generally holds fast to the single point of view in her short stories, does cross over from view to view in her novella *Gate of Ivory, Gate of Horn*, while in her novels *Carnival for the Gods* and *Ghost Dance*, she ranges widely to great effect amongst two circusfuls of viewpoints.

It would be foolish to take a fast, dogmatic position on the subject. What works sometimes in some place might be poison elsewhere. Yet once we are aware of this technical aspect of fiction, we are as incapable of summarily dismissing it as we are of refilling a tube of toothpaste.

When point of view shifts, we see it, and when se see it, we ask ourselves, "Why did he do that?" *He.* The author. Intrusion.

As Booth points out, we no longer dwell in that garden of innocence in which people read the Bible, the gospels, ostensibly objective histories, never wondering how the author could so freely make "illicit entries into private minds." Since the disciples were all asleep, who heard Christ ask his Father to "let this cup pass"? How would we react if a *Time* journalist purported to enter the mind or heart of the president of the United States when even Robley Wilson, Jr., in a chilly postmodern fiction like "Saying Goodbye to the President," holds meticulously to the first person narrator's point of view, never viewing the president from anywhere but outside his skin? Here, no doubt, Professor Gass would remind us that characters in fiction do not have skin; they have words and words only.

Obviously, there are many points of view on point of view. When I was attending writing courses and workshops, there seemed a general fiat against *ever* shifting point of view; one did so at one's peril. I can recall arguing in vain on behalf of a very fine story with a double point of view; the workshop moderator — himself an accomplished writer — was adamant. One story, one point of view; split the point of view and you puncture the story's bladder. I was pleased to see the story eventually win a prize, which of course proves nothing so much as that the contest judge shared my opinion of it. Still the instructor's insistence puzzled me, for I knew many wonderful novels employed multiple point of view, and I had seen the technique used, in my opinion, very successfully in short stories as well by fine writers like Harold Jaffe, Andre Dubus, W. D. Wetherell, and for that matter James Joyce.

On this background, it seemed to me that a survey of the problem might be useful for writer and reader alike. Therefore, I circulated my thoughts on the matter to a number of writers who also teach writing and edit literary journals, with the hope of trying, if not to find an answer, at least to clarify the questions and issues involved. Following are the comments I received.

135

ANDRE DUBUS (1937-99), fiction writer

"I know we all learned this as kids. Then when I was in Iowa, I said to Dick Yates something about you can't split the point of view, and he said, 'Why?' I didn't have an answer. I was about twenty-eight then. He split up point of view a lot in his stories. I do it when another character suddenly grabs me by the sleeve and says, 'I want to talk.'"

SUSAN M. DODD, fiction writer

"You say, 'It would be foolish to take a fast, dogmatic position...' and you are right, of course. But I have one fast dogmatic position on this: *shifting point of view works when it is essential to the work and falls flat when it is simply convenient to the author.* When it is 'essential' — in the most literal sense, of the work's essence — then it has the effect of deepening, accruing power. When it is just 'convenient,' even if it is nervy, flashy, clever, it has the effect of dissipation. I've just finished (relative term) my second novel, *Mawmaw* (a fictional bio of Zerelda Samuel, the mother of Frank and Jesse James), in which I use a constantly and widely shifting point of view. I believe that the nature of the material I was dealing with in this book *demanded* that treatment...and I discovered that the hard way: after writing the first 200 pages in first person. The nature of the events themselves (chaotic, often violent), the nature of the protagonist (passionate, highly unreliable, eventually half-mad), and one of the themes of the book (the indistinguishable merging of history/myth, fact/legend)...all these factors intrinsic to the work itself really seemed to *dictate* (though I didn't pay attention to it at first) that the reader: a) be brought up very close, but b) be given the most reliable possible position. Objective omniscience would have been too distanced, I think...what was wanted, then, it seemed to me, was the sort of realiability Faulkner provides in *As I Lay Dying* — the pastiche of experience a reader can get from walking a mile in *everybody's* shoes...then being permitted to distill those varied experiences into a single personal (reader's) impression...in a way, isn't this the most objective technique of all...and a very good way for authorial intrusion to be kept out of things? With the pastiche, a writer is almost forced to give 'equal time' (evenhanded treatment) to a character's dream, a Pinkerton report, historical fact about the Bush-whackers, dramatic action, spoken word...like a cinematographer, one has the chance to 'shoot from every angle'."

PATRICK SAMWAY, S.J., author, editor

"A good deal of writing has been done on this topic, especially by the French who love arrows and circles and squares to track the various speakers in a given work. But generally, works of literature that embody multiple points of view remind us that Truth is composed of many truths, that realities are not static and contained, but in process, constantly being nuanced and modified, and out there to be discovered over and over again. All writers use multiple points of view, unless their eyes are fixed permanently so that they cannot help but stare straight ahead. The question then becomes: How does a specific writer incorporate various viewpoints into his or her work of fiction so that they contribute to the success of the work? Faulkner's *As I Lay Dying*, for example, is a novel that fragments many times the four parts of *The Sound and the Fury* as it creates a chorus of voices — some internal, some external — recounting the death and burial of Addie Bundren. To a large extent, the novel is held together by a web of eye contact as one or another of the characters (sometimes off stage) looks at another character and thinks about the person envisioned. And in integrating the novel's cubistic design that is a result of the sequence of short chapters, which is made manageable by the linear development as we follow the funeral cortège to Jefferson, we readers are forced to co-create with the author as we interiorize the story at any given point and rearrange the structure so the story makes good human sense. Thus, one

137

result of Faulkner's use of multiple viewpoints in this novel is that the reader in order to finish the novel, must make a definite commitment to the text and work with (or against) the text in order to assimilate what is going on. One could even say that because of the difficult structure of this novel, Faulkner himself chooses his readers, rather than the other way around. A few words about *As I Lay Dying* can hardly do justice to the complexity of this text and the multiple voices and views present. More extended comments could and need to be made about this text and about the entire Faulkner canon — and the spaces in between: the intertexts — in order to begin to see the manifold ways that Faulkner deals with the techniques and problems associated with viewpoints in his fiction. From this perspective, one could then develop a methodology based on a reading of the texts of other American and foreign authors that likewise accounts for similarities and differences of these authors until a point is reached through a process of induction that an argument could be articulated that presses out tentative Truth (always subject to revision and modification as more evidence is deduced) from the truths discovered in the authors studied. Once this is done, then one should take even more seriously how others would deal with the same problematic, and profit from their thoughts."

SHARON SHEEHE STARK, fiction writer

In my novel *A Wrestling Season*, Louise Kleeve tells her friend Frank, '...all my ideas die, in time, of stupidity or boredom.' Funny she and I should think so much alike. I don't begin a story with set notions of anything including point of view. When the work is done, I go on to develop these extremely byzantine and elliptical, impossible-to-follow hypotheses to justify whatever whichway I did it. How sneaky of me. If I get any more flexible, I'll have to be bottled to keep me in one spot. For *real* advice, go directly to Gordon Weaver.

GORDON WEAVER, fiction writer, founding editor of *Mississippi Review*, former editor of *Cimarron Review*.

It strikes me here there are two factors, one aesthetic, one psychological (or epistemological), that need to be considered in any discussion of point of view in fiction. First, all art, including literature, is premised on the basic value of unity; at its best, art presents its audience with a unity (a cosmos, as it were) more whole and symmetrical than is to be found in 'reality.' Aestheticians have worried unity in literature over the centuries from Aristotle onward; in dramatic unities sometimes the discussions have been silly (the classical dramatic unities for example), sometimes instructive. Point of view is simply one of the possible loci of unity in a fiction. Unity of point of view will not guarantee the success of a fiction, but can add to that desired effect (which of course predates Poe in aesthetics), can contribute to an overall unity created in a variety of fictional aspects (narrative, language/style/voice, imagery, etc.) To shift viewpoint arbitrarily, for the author's convenience (to provide exposition for instance), is to jeopardize the very basis of art, which lies in the principled exercise of the medium's conventions. So much for the aesthetic argument in favor of a unified point of view. More basic, related to how we can know what we think we know, unity of point of view comes again into play. For a fiction's audience to have any fixed position against which to measure (and so understand and interpret) what is presented, that audience (reader) has to remain in a stable posture. If viewpoint shifts, no matter how self-conscious and princpled their justifications, are too frequent, and the duration over which a given viewpoint prevails is insufficient, the audience's (reader's) attention may shift from what is presented to how it is being presented. This can be a legitimate intention (self-reflexive fiction), but taken to an extreme, a rapid stream of viewpoint shifts can be as disconcerting as it would be to be forced to change your seat in a theater every fifteen minutes — you're left wondering where you are, or where you should be, or yearning for where you were half an hour ago.

What's on stage is relegated to minor importance.

Axioms are probably impossible in fiction (once you accept the arbitrary symbol system that is language itself), and guidelines proven in practice seem always open to successful violation. I would argue that the shorter a given fiction, the less possible it is to successfully change viewpoint, but Joyce's "The Boarding House" employs three viewpoints (one shift coming at the very end of the story) to great advantage. The trick is that Joyce has a very broad unity in that story achieved via his omniscient narrative persona.

In the end, it's well to keep in mind that point of view is not a value, it's a convention, a way of doing something, an element of fictional form. And in fictions, form succeeds or fails only and always in the linguistic/semantic context of the example under scrutiny."

W. D. WETHERELL, fiction writer

"I'd like to write from multiple points of view more, am always telling myself to, but almost invariably — with a story — end up sticking to the one story teller. With the same inspiration that brings me a story idea comes the person telling the story and it's hard to divide this flash into two or three. The one story where I think I was successful with multiple points of view, 'If a Woodchuck Could Chuck Wood' (in *The Man Who Loved Levitown*) was a story about the interrelationship of three generations, and so selecting a member of each generation to tell their share of the story seemed very natural. I suspect many people write from multiple points of view as a sort of compromise — they can't decide who rightly tells the story, and so hedge — but done effectively, it can widen a story's range. What I seem to be doing a lot lately is sticking with the single point of view, but finding ways of including healthy chunks of another character's perspectives; hence, in 'Hundred Year War' (in *Hyanns Boat*), the story is told from the perspective of a Vietnamese cabbie in

Washington, D.C., but there are large sections of first person transmission over the two-way radio from the character's alter-ego, a Vietnam vet missing a leg who acts as the cab company's dispatcher. I do something similar in 'The Next Sound You Hear' (*Hyanns Boat*) where a classical music DJ tells the story, but we get long abusive memos from his enemy, a rock-and-roll DJ who works the day shift. This may be having your cake and eating it, too, but it seems natural to me and I suspect I trust this method more since it doesn't require the intellectual tightrope walking multiple points of view sometimes requires."

Although arranging alphabetically the responses which I received to my query might seem an arbitrary way to assemble them, having done so, it seems to me that a meaningful collage of views on this topic emerges, a shifting attitude from professional impatience to incisive discourse to a blithe refusal to worry such a point to a relaxed consideration of how one has, oneself, handled this problem. Reading the replies in this order seems to me to reflect the variety of valid positions to be taken; in a sense, perhaps every writer must contain *all* of these attitudes toward the problem - much in the way that Fitzgerald suggested a first-rate intelligence needs to be able to hold two or more opposing ideas while continuing to function, or as Whitman proclaimed: *I am complex! I contain contradictions!*

Finally, however, I would be remiss and would scant the subjects of voice, narrative persona, point of view, and authorial presence by leaving it at this.

Modern or contemporary styles of fiction tend to attempt to reduce the sense of artificiality in a fiction by reducing the sense of authorial presence via the employment of such conventions as that of strict point of view manipulation (unless they seek to circumvent the reader's awareness of illusion and artificiality by an apparent authorial intrusion in fact aimed at winning the reader's belief that the author's intrusion is smashing artificial conventions by stepping in to kick them aside — the illusion-shattering illusion discussed previously.)

However, as Wayne C. Booth says in *The Rhetoric of Fiction*, even with conventionally identifiable "forms of author's voice expunged, what we have left will reveal to us a shameful artificiality." As William H. Gass puts it, "Storytelling is as artificial as baked Alaska."

But, Booth goes on, "The author's judgement is always present, always evident to anyone who knows how to look for it...we must never forget that though the author can to some extent choose his disguises, he can never choose to disappear."

Narrative persona is complicated by the fact that first person persona combines voice *and* viewpoint and third person persona allows for a whole range of possibilities of voice and any number of distances between persona and viewpoint character in third person. Further, multiple first person personae in a fiction differ from shifts in omniscience (third person and viewpoint).

Those interested in a deep and comprehensive study of such points are referred to Booth who, while he notes that "we students of literature can never become as scientific as our forebears hoped," does seem to me to have produced a book on the art as near science as it might come, even in an age when the new physics seems to have embraced a science of Blakean imagination.

ASKING QUESTIONS

Years ago I saw a painting that depicted a monk at his desk writing while a lion stands on its hind legs against the chairback to peer over the monk's shoulder, eyes wide with fascination at the mysterious activity of quill on page. I do not remember where I saw this or what it was from, other than that the lion had that medieval look of inaccuracy — perhaps not many painters had actually *seen* a lion then. What I particularly liked about the picture was that it represented not a fascination merely with a text, but with the process of creating a text, the art, the act, *and* the actor.

As a young reader of fiction, I enthusiastically welcomed Holden Caulfield's statement in J. D. Salinger's *Catcher in the Rye* that certain books, when you finish them, make you wish you could call up and talk to the author.

As a young writer of fiction, I became more specific and urgent in the yearning. I began to read interviews with writers and books on the craft of fiction by writers whose work I admired. By chance then, in a second-hand bookstore in Copenhagen owned by an expatriate American, I came upon an old college text called *Understanding Fiction* by Cleanth Brooks and Robert Penn Warren, an excellent book, which if it is not still in print, ought to be. Among its pages is a brief essay by John Cheever entitled "What Happened," in which he discusses how he came to write his wonderful story, "Goodbye, My Brother."

In the essay, Cheever talks about the mix of elements which went into the writing of the story. I have quoted from this in a pervious chapter, but the statement in its full is worthy of recapitulation:

> "I know almost no pleasure greater than having a piece of fiction draw together incidents as disparate as a dance in Minneapolis and a backgammon game in the mountains so that they relate to one another and confirm the feeling that life itself is creative process, that one thing is put purposefully upon another, that what is lost in one encounter is replenished in the next and that we possess some power to make sense of what takes place."

He further states, "You can pick and choose from a wide range of memory, picking the smell of roses from a very different place and the ringing of a tennis court roller that you heard years ago," and that when a writer pushes open a fictional door to a fictional kitchen, he may well discover there a cook who had worked for his mother years before.

This, of course, is another way of speaking of what Coleridge called the esemplastic power of the imagination — the capability of forging unity out of diversity.

Cheever's essay was a startling revelation for me. It had answered a question I had not yet managed to phrase. Somehow I had been laboring under the delusion that a fiction writer must make everything up. If I borrowed something from my own life, I feared I was cheating. Worse, if I incorporated something that occurred even as I was writing (as once when my secretary interrupted me during a writing session to tell me an anecdote of something that had happened to her son, and when I went back to my writing, I found the anecdote incorporated in my story-in-progress), I felt like a fraud.

Cheever's essay helped free me from that misconception as did at least three other outstanding works of metafiction, mentioned elsewhere in this book already, but I will repeat their titles nevertheless: Sherwood Anderson's "Death in the Woods,"

Gordon Weaver's "The Parts of Speech," and Francois Camoin's "Diehl: The Wandering Years" — in each of which the process I am discussing here becomes a surface and thematic element open to view and intrinsically involved in the story.

As I began to get more serious about writing, I found myself posing difficult questions about what I read. First I asked myself these questions, but found that I had more questions than answers. I wanted to know not only *what* does this story mean or even only *how* does it mean, but rather how and why and in what context, on the background of what reflection and by which process did it come to take the form and content with which the process of its creation ended, the final product. Questions impossible to answer in full, for every answer leads to more questions, but still it seemed it must be possible to gain insights into the process in the variety of its practice.

So I got the idea of asking the authors themselves. I also began to write essays and reviews whose aim was to explain to myself what I understood of what I was reading. To my surprise, I found that process to be not only a recapitulation of the creative act of the author in question — Poe's "kindred art" — but also a creative act on my part. I had to create explanations for what was there on the page, even if those explanations were little more than a series of questions based upon uncertain assumptions — or uncertain assumptions based upon unanswered questions.

Usually the reader is alone in this process. Sometimes she or he has the help of a critic. But I was like Holden Caulfield. I wanted to phone the writer and talk to him or her about it: Why did you do that? What did you mean by that? Why does your story end *there*? What did the story mean to *you*? And then it occurred to me that nothing was stopping me from doing just that. Perhaps not phoning, but at least writing a letter, setting forth my questions, going to readings and approaching the reader afterwards to propose an interview. Even if J. D. Salinger himself was not amenable to satisfying the desire that he put into the heart of his character — many a prospective Salinger interviewer

145

has discovered this, even Greg Herriges who came the closest of all of them, allowed into Salinger's garage for ten minutes on the solemn promise not to have a tape recorder or pad and pencil with him (see www.herriges.com) — still I found that most other writers, in fact all but three of the fifty plus writers I approached, were quite open to such an approach. Most writers are happy to talk about their work.

Over the years then I conducted full-scale interviews with fifteen or more writers and in attempting to explain their fiction to myself produced perhaps half a hundred essays and reviews, all of which were ultimately published and grew into three published books as well as two recent anthologies in which forty-three writers kindly wrote essays about how one of their stories or poems came to be written. It was a further source of delight that my attempts to satisfy my own intellectual and creative curiosity could prove a source of additional revenue as well as that there were editors interested in publishing the results. A confirmation of the validity of my ignorance and value of my attempts to satisfy it.

More important to me, however, than the publication of or payment for these texts was what I learned researching, conducting and writing them.

When I began to ask these questions and think more deeply about the fictions I was reading, the fictions I wished to write began to take clearer form, began to assume a wholeness of some sort, and I began more clearly to comprehend what I was attempting to do as a story writer.

There was a time that my critical publications outweighed my fiction ones, which came close to starting an identity crisis. I began to wonder if I was really a writer at all; perhaps I was only a person with a lot of questions, a very curious reader. But that proved to be only in the beginning, a reflection of the early learning process. The critical investigations — the questions I asked — proved ultimately a powerful fuel for my fiction.

Not every writer I approached was happy to explain the

sources of their stories or poems. With an anthology I guest-edited for *The Literary Review* entitled *Poems & Sources* (published in Fall 2000, a companion volume to *Stories & Sources*, published two years earlier), three of the participating poets — John Updike, Charles Simic, and Albert Goldbarth — questioned the value of providing "explanations" of their poems.

What has this to do with "the proper power and beckon of someone's poem?" Albert Goldbarth asked. I don't know. But I then invited Messrs. Updike, Goldbarth, and Simic to provide brief explanations of why they did *not* wish to explain the background of their pieces, and even these I find useful to the reader seeking a glimpse into the process.

After all, statements by writers on the art of literature have always helped readers to come closer to the work, even if the statement concerns the impossibility of comprehension, or necessity of incomprehension. I think of Keats's negative capability, how the poet must be "capable of being in uncertainties, mysteries, doubts, without any irritable reaching after fact and reason." Yet the fact of that statement provides clarity and strength with which to face the uncertainty.

So, too, Rilke's statement — already quoted in an earlier chapter but which bears repeating — on the futility of criticism paradoxically helps expand the critical faculty:

> "With nothing can one approach a work of art so little as with critical words: they always come down to more or less happy misunderstandings. Things are not all so comprehensible and expressible as one would mostly have us believe; most events are inexpressible, taking place in a realm which no word has ever entered, and more inexpressible than all else are works of art, mysterious existences the life of which, while ours pass away, endures."

With the *Stories & Sources* and *Poems & Sources* anthologies, I also requested photographs of the participating authors. Albert

Goldbarth sent me one of himself with a note: "The photo you requested is enclosed. Not that I blame you for wanting to spice up the issue with such stuffs, and not that I have a major self-image in always being Mr. Churlish, but — what *has* any of this to do with the proper power and beckon of someone's poem?"

A strong question and a good one. I do not know the answer. I only know that *everything* about stories and poems continues to hold me in its trance like a fascinated beast; even if wanting more than only the story or the poem might seem beside the point of the work itself, I will continue to want more. I will eat the text and the commentary, too, gobble down the bio notes and proceed to the photos, peering intently at the reflected faces of the writers for whatever else I might find there.

My advice, then, is not to underestimate the power of a hungering ignorance. Sometimes the deep ache of wanting to know something can be relieved with a question.

THE WATER THAT WEARS AWAY THE STONE: WEATHERING REJECTION

"The waters wear the stones."
— Job 14:9

We regret that the volume of submissions is such that we must use this printed form to notify you that after careful consideration we have decided your submission does not meet our current editorial needs
—The Editors.

What could be more discouraging than an impersonal, anonymous, unsigned, printed rejection form returning the story or poem you have labored so hard to bring forth, from the first glimmer of vision to a final, structured, polished work of linguistic art so unremarkable the editors didn't even care to comment. Just lifted a form from a shelf (*Sorry, this piece is not for us...*), yawned, slid it in under the paper clip on the manuscript, shoved the whole thing into your SASE, and shot it back to you. Over the transom, into the slush pile, out the door.

This form does not necessarily reflect upon the quality of your work. We say this to nearly everybody.

That awful moment of loneliness, alone with the anonymously returned manuscript. You read it, see it with the eyes of the unknown, sphinx-like strangers who have chucked it back at you, see through it at last. Its small suspected flaws suddenly flare up and glare at you like enflamed boils. You blush, ashamed, fling the thing into a bottom drawer, and slam it shut, feeling *sick* about all the time you wasted, about the shameful hungering ego that drives you to try to distinguish yourself, to expose yourself like this. You look into the mirror, catch yourself in this weakness, eyes full of naked lust to see your name in print, your words in type with justified right margins on acid-free paper, maybe with your name on the cover as well, mentioned by the editor of the journal in his or her preface... You could barf at the sight of yourself. *Give it up, phony. Stop wasting your time. You are nobody, nothing, and that's all you'll ever be. You and your feeble ideas, your skinny so-called talent, your — ha! — visions! Hang it up. Quit.*

But you can't quit. You won't. You can't. You have already read Rainer Maria Rilke's *Letters to a Young Poet*, have already asked yourself the question posed by the master: Must I do this? Must I write? And you already have answered: Yes. I must.

You are one of us for whom writing is an obsession, a vocation, a mania even.

It is amazing the amount of rejection a writer can take, the number of years she or he will labor with little or no reward or encouragement, the number of rejections that can be weathered on a single piece without giving up.

Gladys Swan wrote fiction for more than twenty years before publishing her first story, then wrote for another seven years after that before publishing her first book, and labored yet another seven years before publishing her second. Yet her faith in her talent in her passion remained strong over those years and earned her a reputation as a writer of uncompromising integrity. By now she has seven volumes of fiction in print and more on the way.

Andre Dubus (1937-1999) said, "I think most writers quit between the ages of twenty and thirty for various reasons... They don't have friends who really understand what they're doing. They don't get published; they work and work and don't get any money for it. There is no one who cares whether they work, no one who can threaten them with firing, no one to set the alarm clock for. And you know, you finally do publish in something as lovely as *Tendrils* or *Ploughshares*...and you call your mother or father and tell them and they say, 'What's that?' So it comes down to that person believing in herself or himself and saying I *will*... It takes an awful lot of courage."

Dubus sent out one story, "Waiting" (a seven-page short story that took fourteen months to write), thirty-eight times before it finally was accepted by a very little magazine. "The manuscript was worn so thin by then," Dubus said, "You could have used it for toilet paper."

Yet that story is part of his canon, has been reprinted many times, is an American story of great distinction.

"This writing game is a paradox," says fiction writer Gordon Weaver. "What temerity, what ego it requires to imagine that anyone could care to read, much less enjoy or profit from reading, anything I or any one else might write! So on the one hand there is an almost sickening self-confidence, on the other, one doubts one can really write anything of worth to communicate to another."

Weaver once sent a story out forty-four times before it finally was taken by a magazine, which proceeded to publish a number of his stories in succession for a generous fee. He also waited a dozen years while Hollywood dangled a movie contract on one of his novels (*Count a Lonely Cadence*) in front of his nose, renewing the option a year at a time while various actors and directors took an interest in, then abandoned, the script; then suddenly, in 1989, just when it looked like nothing would ever happen, he received a fat check in the mail and news that the film had gone into production, directed by Martin Sheen, starring Martin and Charlie Sheen — ultimately issued as *Cadence*.

I myself was at it for nearly twenty years before placing my first story — in a magazine that went out of business with the issue in which my story appeared. I published my second story the same year; the *acceptance* letter was a printed form with my name penned in. It included an offer to sell me a T-shirt emblazoned with an announcement that the magazine had published me. I might even have purchased the shirt, except that given the name of the magazine, the T-shirt was rather unfortunate: *Nit & Wit Published Me.* I truly felt like a nitwit. But the year after, I published what I think of as my first "real" story, for which I was paid twenty dollars and which won me my first agent, and things began to move faster.

And in the years since, I've published many books, stories, poems, essays, translations. A few of the journals with which I had had repeated contact began to ask *me* for advice — a thing that caught me quite by surprise and gave me the opportunity to see things from the other side of the fence as well. Consequently I serve and have served editorial functions with numerous literary journals.

In these roles, I have come to see that a sense of dead certainty about one's decision is not a frequent editorial experience. This is one of the challenges of being an editor, reading and rereading a work, to try to measure whether the initial enthusiasm or the initial skepticism it has inspired holds water. An editorial decision is not always easy. I once was contacted by an editor a year after he had rejected one of my stories to ask if it was still available; he had been thinking about it for a year and had finally given in to it. I had the pleasure of informing him it was already published and had, in fact, won a Pushcart Prize.

Poet Jack Myers tells how by the time he was twenty-seven he "decided to defy the main thrust of editorial opinion by literally wallpapering my study with hundreds of rejection slips. I laughed and challenged the censorius atmosphere for a month or so..." Then one day, Myers was struck by the "depressing futility of it all. I seemed to have made a decor of failure more sturdy than my Pollyanna will to succeed. Soon I took the slips down, saved them in a box, transferred them to a larger box, then threw it all out. I have persisted mainly because I have to write and want to publish what I've written."

I tried for years to save my rejection slips because it seemed to me a part of the sociology of the whole thing and I still have many of them. I don't want to forget how much effort has gone into writing. I also want to remember those many editors: those who shot me down without so much as a faintly pencilled "Sorry"; those who said kind of silly or presumptuous things like, "I know you will be very disappointed to receive this rejection..." Like, hey, it's okay, I'll survive. Those who offered advice of a useful, indifferent, or ludicrous nature; and the many kind, busy editors who took the trouble to encourage me along the way on the basis of manuscripts some of which make me curl my toes with embarrassment to look at today. In fact, I've thrown out some of the manuscripts and saved the rejection notes instead.

Others still have offered advice that no doubt was meant to set me straight (cold water in the face of a man suffering raving delusions), but tended to get me giggling or, on one occasion, brought me near apoplexy. The editor of a distinguished old-line journal once responded to my fourth or fifth submission by telling me it was most unlikely that he would ever publish anything I wrote and advising me, therefore, to aim for "less major fora" where I might stand a better chance of seeing print.

A poet friend suggested that anyone who would use the term "less major fora," no doubt slept in a bowtie, but I was mad. I have a policy of not responding to rejection notes, but this one! "I *have* to answer this!" I said to my wife. "What can I tell him!?"

She said, "Send him something else."

What a mind! I did that, and the editor wrote back, saying, "You are relentless, Mr. Kennedy," and lectured me for a page on my slipshod writing habits, but he wound up accepting the piece and the next piece I sent him as well. In fact both of those pieces were reprinted in anthologies not long ago.

Not everyone is opposed to rejections. Poet Mark Cox (*Smoulder*, Godine, 1989) says, "Anything that speeds up the process is fine by me." Apparently he prefers a printed rejection form that comes fast to comments like, "These are not complete enough for me," with which one editor personalized one of his rejection slips. He professes not even to mind getting rejected ("now that I have been accepted") except that "it takes some editors so goddamn long to do it." Now, however, he is director of a university writing program with several books to his credit, so these reminiscences from the start of his career can be seen in another perspective.

The length of time it sometimes takes is, of course, a major administrative problem in trying to get your work into print while it is still new enough to you that you care about it. If an editor sits on your work for half a year or more, the energy with which you intially took it to the market begins to dissipate.

Unfortunately the length of time a piece is held is no indication of anything; I've had pieces accepted fast and rejected slow, and vice versa. Probably most writers have waited three or four months on a piece and queried to learn that it was never received or that the journal is no longer in business or that the logbook shows it was returned eight weeks ago or that the journal is so seriously backlogged that they will not be reading again until next year. I've had pieces held for more than a year with suggestions for revision that I complied with one or more times and which ended finally in rejection anyway, and I have been courted sometimes for several years by editors who never did publish me after all. Others who rejected my work recommended me to journals that accepted it. Sometimes, inexplicably, a personal relationship with an editor has suddenly devolved into printed rejection slips again. And sometimes I have decided never again to submit to a journal because of their slipshod manner of handling manuscripts.

Personal rejection notes may be instructive, encouraging, annoying, off-the-wall, or entertainingly ludicrous. When this article was published originally in different form in *Poets & Writers*, it attracted numerous letters to the editor including one from an editor scolding me for suggesting that an editor's comments could *ever* be considered ludicrous. How droll!

But most important with a personally written rejection note, in my opinion, is that they give you some sense of the human beings out there to whom you are submitting your work. And you begin to understand that many of them are more or less like yourself — fallible, overworked, underpaid, passionately involved with literature, and often uncertain of what is good, having to rely finally on the old ground line of *Okay, maybe it's art, but do I like it?* A rejection does not invalidate your story — any more than an acceptance necessarily affirms its worth. Even getting your work published is no guarantee of its being read. Sure, the editor reads it, but how many others? Two? Ten? Fifty people? Okay, if you're appearing in *The New Yorker* or *Playboy* those numbers will be greater, but even then most of your work will not be appearing in mass markets. "Ultimately, you reach only a very few people with even your best shot," says Jack Myers.

Why do we keep on then? Even if you establish your credentials with a long list of impressive credits, you are not likely to be one of the fortunate few who manage to make more than a supplementary income out of it. Even a bestseller is not sure to net you much more than, say, the equivalent of a year's salary for a middle-level executive, aside from what you can bank on sideshows — readings, lectures, etc. I've had reading fees that paid better than advances on book contracts and they are often better than what you get from a literary journal for one time rights on the very story you read.. Or as Andre Dubus once pointed out, with the three thousand dollars you get from *The New Yorker* for a story, you can't run away to Mexico to write. Even twenty thousand dollars from the National Endowment for the Arts is not going to stretch all that far in today's supermarket. And if you hit the jackpot and get a genius award, fifty thousand dollars a year for five years or whatever, you have to promise to drop any other jobs you have and when those five years are over, who is to ensure that you will be in an economically viable situation? I was once offered two years as writer in residence for fifty grand a year where I would have few obligations other than to write, but with a family and house and other financial obligations in Denmark, I had to say no.

So why do we do it? Because we can't quit. Why can't we quit? Because we're writers. And what is a writer? Gordon Weaver's definition, in my opinion, says it all:

"A writer is one who writes; a serious writer is one who writes as well as he or she can as consistently as possible and for whom writing is the most serious activity he or she knows. How much money, fame, or publication comes of it — these are extra-literary factors."

II. STORIES & SOURCES: TWO STORIES AND HOW THEY WERE WRITTEN

INTRODUCTION

As I explain elsewhere in this book, one of the most valuable early lessons I Iearned when I was beginning at fiction I found in the book *Understanding Fiction* edited by Cleanth Brooks and Robert Penn Warren. One section of that book included a group of four stories followed by a statement by the author telling how the stories came to be written.

These explanations were of great value to me — far greater than the cryptic, often seemingly moronic "questions for study" one encountered as an undergraduate in the anthologies employed for literary survey courses, questions which invariably seemed to me harder to comprehend than the stories themselves.

Inspired by the Brooks and Warren book, I went on, years later, to edit two anthologies of my own, also mentioned elsewhere in this book: *Stories & Sources* and *Poems & Sources*, published as special issues of *The Literary Review* (Fall 1998 and Fall 2000).

The pleasure and enlightenment I enjoyed in putting together those anthologies reconfirmed for me the value for a writer of being afforded a glimpse into another writer's processes in creating a story or a poem.

Thus, I am offering here, in the hope that it might be of interest and of use, a glimpse into what led me to write two of my own stories and the way in which, the extent to which, and the point at which I myself began to understand what was happening as the stories unfolded for me.

I have chosen two styles of story — one that is more or less surrealistic, another that is more or less realistic — and I have tried to comment on as many aspects of the process of their creation as I could recall. They are from two different collections and were written approximately six years apart.

WHAT DOES GOD CARE ABOUT YOUR DIGNITY, VICTOR TRAVESTI?

"Happy is the man whom God correcteth;
therefore despise not thou
the chastening of the Almighty."
Eliphaz:Job:5:17

Victor Travesti stood beneath the bus shelter, tall, hands easy in the slash pockets of his trenchcoat. The coat hung open on him, exhibiting the hand-stitched lapels of his silver suit. He watched for the bus, thinking ruefully of the copper Mercedes XL25 which Jewish people had sent an ape to take from him.

Seated on the bench at his back, two women in their late sixties chatted. Rain drizzled from the grey sky onto the pavement and slicked the road.

"It's sad for all the little boys who wanted to play ball today," one of the women said.

Let them drown, thought Victor Travesti, watching for his bus.

"And just think of all the families who planned to go on picnics," the other woman said.

"Such a shame."

Let them eat grief, thought Victor.

The broad glass face of the bus appeared at the corner. The vehicle slid in alongside the curb, wheezed to a halt, clapped open its doors. Victor Travesti turned and with his arm swept a gallant, imaginary path toward the bus to usher the women ahead of him.

"Ladies," he said, and bowed to them.

"Such charms," said one. The other giggled, fluttered her eyelashes, plumped up her thin, red-black hair. "Sidney Omar said my stars showed a tall dark handsome fella," she said.

"Your Stars Today," pronounced the first dreamily, with a smile of mystical ignorance.

Victor Travesti winked, poker-faced. Then his strong white teeth flashed as he guided the ladies up the steps of the bus, averting his eyes from the rolling masses of their flowered backsides.

"My mother always said to beware the Latin charm," the balding red-headed woman said, glancing sidewise and up into Victor's dark face, which replied with graceful forebearance.

Yes, he had charm. And scorn, too. He knew how much hand to give, and to whom, and how. For the upstart, for the Irish fornicator, two fingers, while the eyes look elsewhere. Full clasp for peers, for men of respect. He had all the tools of a good *paysan*. His people had been *Calabrese*. He thought it sad that a man of his dignity should have to ride the public bus with balding old ladies.

The reek of a rainy Saturday hung over the seats and passengers inside the bus — wet corduroy, yesterday's onions, breath. Victor Travesti sat by a window and watched the streets and neighborhoods of Queens roll past. Corona, Jackson Heights, Woodside, Sunnyside, the chintzy optimism of a people who would call their main road "Bliss Street." He watched the shops and houses and apartment buildings of people who were doing better than he, people whose dusty shoe shops and drycleaners hung on, decade after decade, despite the neglect and sloth of their owners, while to Victor, who rose early and worked hard and bore himself with the dignity of a *Calabrese*, fate had dealt failure as a crown upon his efforts.

Victor Travesti signalled his stop and rose, thinking of his wife and two boys and the Irishman who now lived with them,

162

sleeping in bed with the woman who had pledged herself to Victor at the altar of God, sharing her marital bed in the same house where his children slept, eating food at the table with them. Victor's family. With whom a court had told Victor he had no right to be except twice a month at a time chosen by the wife who had violated her pledge. This they called justice. A woman spends afternoons in secret meetings, becomes drunken in public in company with a lecherous man in a business suit, and the court gives to her Victor Travesti's sons.

The judge had been a Jew. Silvermann. A tuft of dark hair jutted from each of Silvermann's nostrils and his eyeglasses had been dirty, speckled with dandruff and grease. When he informed the family of his decision concerning the fate of Victor Travesti's sons, Victor had clamped his jaws tight and risen. He had gazed upon the woman and her Irish lawyer in his shiny three-piece suit, forced them to observe the smouldering of his eyes, his dignity in the face of indignation. He raised his index finger to his eye and smartly drew down the underside of the eyelid: I see this outrage. I see your deceit. Victor Travesti sees.

Things had not gone well for Victor Travesti. Tribulation was upon him. His business had failed. He had had to go out begging to work for other men, companies. Victor Travesti had had to offer his skills and wisdom for money, payable by the hour, by the day, the week, to offer himself as a laborer in another man's vineyard, and even that was denied him. No one was left whom he even could beg. He had had to return to live again as a boy in the house of his mother. To see his sons, he had to ride in a public bus and wait with his hat in his hand in the foyer of the Irish fornicator who had cheated him of his family. A man named Sweeney with green creases between his teeth and the red veins of drunkeness across his nose.

The bus slowed. One of the old ladies, moving toward the rear doors, weaved off balance. Victor Travesti's hand leapt to her aid, steadied her by the elbow. She fluttered her eyelids at him. He nodded, dealt her a small, firm smile, held her elbow while she descended before him to the street.

The instant's delay which his courtesy produced decided the course of the brief remainder of Victor Travesti's life.

As he stepped off the bus, he heard a strange sound, very slight, yet somehow foreboding, a kind of hiss, a plop, and there was something familiar and strangely taunting in the sound. He heard the wings of a bird shiver overhead, the mocking scream of a gull, as he stood at the curb, hands in the slash pockets of his trenchcoat. Two men standing beside a carpet truck laughed raucously. Lettered on the side of the truck were the words Kipling Karpet Ko. The men were thick and red-faced. The one smoked a cigarette and smirked. The other wheezed with laughter. Pointing a thick hair-knuckled finger at Victor Travesti, he said, "I want to sing like the boidies do, tweet tweet tweet."

Victor Travesti clamped his jaws shut. The old woman he had helped off the bus was pushing a fistful of tissues at him.

"You poor dear," she said, "Don't you pay them no mind." She daubed at the lapel of his raincoat. Victor Travesti tipped his chin toward his throat and strained his eyes to see. Something green and white was sketched down its front. Victor grimaced, looked about him with chill fury. The red-faced man stood with his palms on his thighs and wheezed.

Victor Travesti took the kleenex roughly from the woman's hand, wiped at his lapel. He pitched the crumpled, slimey paper into a refuse basket, shook his hands as though to shed water, fumbled into his pocket for his handkerchief. The stuff was streaked on the lapel of his silver suit as well as on his Sardinian silk tie.

The old woman was shoving more kleenex at him.

"Please!" he snapped, palming her hand away from him.

"Well!" she said. "Some people."

The hand-stitched lapel of his silver suit was blemished with an ugly stain even after he had scrubbed it with his handkerchief, spit on it, scrubbed more. He could carry the raincoat over his arm, but the jacket and tie were just as bad, worse.

The carpetman watched with unconcealed pleasure. Victor Travesti looked at his freckled, pugged nose, his sandy-red, close-cropped hair. The man seemed to be laughing on behalf of all of Victor Travesti's enemies and tormentors: Judge Silvermann, the Irish fornicator, his adulterous wife, those who had taken over his business, those who had forced him to demean himself requesting permission to labor for their enterprises at a wage and then sent him away with no work. The blood raced to his face, his temples. A brilliant pain seared his skull.

Victor Travesti stood his full height and gazed with chill ferocity from the one carpetman to the other. The smirking one shrugged his shoulders and turned away, but the thick, red-faced man met Victor's gaze with a fury of his own. Victor found it necessary to avert his eyes, to turn away and walk from them.

A bitter taste rose to his mouth as he heard the man speak viciously to his back. "That's right, Salvatori, just keep walkin. That's what ginzos are good at: walkin."

"And fartin," the other added.

"Yeah, that's right. And fartin."

Victor's face burnt with shame. It was difficult for a man of culture and dignity to deal with rabble. Personally, he felt no shame over it, but he had begun to imagine how his sons might have felt had they witnessed the mockery of these orangutans. That they were strangers frightened him vaguely. That strangers should laugh in his face, select him as their target. Why? On what basis?

He remembered the woman at the bus stop with her smile of weird, dreamy ignorance: Your Stars Today. He kept walking, quickened his pace toward a sign in pale red neon script that said, Fortune Dry Cleaners — French Method. Inside, a tall Negro in a white short-sleeved shirt worked the presser, while a man in a lavender mohair sweater did paperwork at the counter.

Victor Travesti laid his coat and jacket on the counter, unknotted his tie and removed it carefully, trying to avoid touching the stain. The man in the mohair sweater took up each garment, examined the stains, laid them gingerly down again. He thrust out his underlip and shook his head. "I don't know about this," he said.

"I need it right away," Victor Travesti said.

The man laughed, tongued the fronts of his upper teeth. "You can have them next Monday."

"I need them now," Victor Travesti said. "As soon as possible."

The man looked at him with a smirk. "I could bulk them for you. You'd have them in a hour. But you'd need to pay a surcharge of twenty-five percent. Standard for a rush job. And no guarantees on that there Eyetalian necktie."

"Do you mean I have to pay a surcharge of twenty-five percent," Victor Travesti asked, "and still get no guarantee?"

The man shrugged. "Take em somewhere else."

"I need them now," Victor Travesti said.

The man said, "The labor's the same whether I succeed or not."

Victor Travesti emptied the pockets of his jacket and coat. He could not allow his wife or the Irish fornicator to see him like this. It would kill him.

"Come back in an hour," the man said and returned to his paperwork.

The Negro drew down the lid of the presser; steam hissed out around the edges.

Outside on the sidewalk, Victor Travesti lit a cigarette. The carpet men were feeding a long rolled-up carpet onto a pile of similarly rolled-up carpets in back of their van. Victor Travesti turned his back on them, walked past an Army & Navy Store, a cake shop, a glass doorway at the foot of a flight of stairs. Lettered across the glass was:

Madame Esth r
Fo tun s
While U Wait
One $/One F ight Up

Victor Travesti looked at his watch, flipped away his cigarette, opened the door. He didn't believe in such superstitious nonsense, although he had an aunt who could predict the weather by flinging drops of scalding olive oil across a scrap of red silk. He just wanted to get off the street, to sit, to have a woman hold his hand and purse her lips and touch his palm with the tips of her fingers and care for a moment or two about his fate. The miraculous medal around his neck jangled as he climbed the wooden staircase two steps at a time.

On the landing were three doors. The first two were locked. He turned the shaky knob of the third and entered a room which was empty but for a ladderback chair in which an old man in a flannel shirt and mustard colored necktie sat gazing out the window. His hair was white and trimmed close at the back and his body looked as though it might once have been powerful, barrel-chested, his hands thick and large, the skin now freckled and puckered with age. The room itself looked as though it were in a building that had been bombed. Plaster had fallen away from the walls in several places, showing the woodwork beneath. The floor was covered with dust and plaster flakes from the ceiling and rubbled with bits of wood and glass, broken bottles, a newspaper which looked as though it had been soaked in water and dried and yellowed in the sun.

"Pardon me," Victor Travesti said. "I was seeking Madame Esther."

The old man said, "I can't even bear to look at it anymore. It's no good. There's no pleasure left in it." He rubbed his eyes with the heels of his hands, then ran a palm over his entire face. "I could as well put it all to the torch." He sighed, clasped his hands across his stomach, closed his eyes. A tubular flesh-colored wart hung from one eyelid.

Victor Travesti waited for a moment to see if the old man would say anything further. He glanced around the room. Apart from the rubble, it was empty. No chair, no other furniture. Against one wall was a gutted yellow plastic radio with a crack in

167

the casing.

As be began to turn away, the old man said, "Shut the door. There's a draft."

Victor Travesti hesitated. "I cannot stay," he said.

"Young men are impatient," the old man said. "It makes them uninterested and therefore uninteresting."

Victor shut the door, put his hands in his pockets, jingled his change, considering how he might amuse himself with this old man. He said, "Thank you for the compliment, sir. In fact, I'm hardly young."

The old man's eyes turned upon him in their pouched lids. "Ha!" he said. "You're all of what? Forty-two."

"Good guess."

The old man snorted, reflected, looked sad. He said, "I had such hopes for you."

Victor Travesti inclined his head in dignified query.

"You were so much greater than the monkies," the old man said. He hawked gravel from his throat, spit it into a handkerchief which he returned to the pocket of his khaki trousers. "The monkies were so stupid," he said. "All they ever did was fiddle with themselves and giggle and throw their crap at each other. Never much cared for the monkies. What can you do with a great ape that does a crosscountry hike just to find some bamboo to chew on? Stupid, vulgar creatures, really. But you," he said and smacked one palm with the back of the other hand. The report was startlingly loud. Victor Travesti flinched, wondered if the old man might get violent. Old as he was, he looked as though he still might have some power in his body, and Victor wasn't in the mood for a confrontation.

"You and all your kind," the old man said. "You had advantages. You had capacities never seen before."

He rose from his chair, crossed to the window, stared down over the elevated train tracks. Without looking from the window, he said, "What good does it do me? What can you do? You try your best, and it all goes bad. Then you start to question your own motives. Who or what was it for? It was sport, too. I was young. It seemed exciting. I liked them to be brave. I liked the men to be brave, and the women to be nubile. They were men, not rodents. I liked them to make spears and run after the tigers." The old man's deep blue eyes lit for a moment, staring into an invisible past which Victor Travesti could see only in the reflection of sudden vivacity on the man's face. "You should have seen them. Three men, naked in the woods, holding big javelins over their heads and chasing one of those great big tigers right through the trees. This was sport: See that big cat go down roaring and the three of them waving those bloody spears in the air, yelling out praises. Praise to the Lord! Hosannah on highest! That's how it was then. That's how it was back then. Once there were such gods..." The old man paused and his eyes grew distant as his mood seemed to slide downward. His eyes were very blue beneath his white eyebrows, his eyesockets deep in sculpted pouches so that his gaze was like a pale blue shadow. The old man sat again, turned his chair toward Victor Travesti.

Victor Travesti's mind had begun to work hard as he listened to the old man's story. Slowly it had begun to occur to him that everything that had happened to him today, all his life, from the instant of his birth, every chance turning and decision, had been leading him to this moment.

When the old man had ceased to speak for some moments, Victor Travesti dug his handkerchief from his pocket, dusted a spot on the bare wood floor. Then he genuflected onto the handkerchief and bowed his head.

"My Lord and my God," Victor Travesti said with humble dignity.

The old man wet his thin purple lips with the tip of his tongue and watched this man on one knee before him.

"Dear Lord," Victor Travesti said. "I have a favor to beg of you. I have been to the courts and have had no satisfaction. My wife is an adulteress, and the man with whom she fornicates has been given to live with my children, my fine young boys, and I can receive no legal satisfaction. Now I am on my way to visit my children, and I cannot let them see me as I am. I must have some clothes. And if I could rent — or buy — a car, could show up in an expensive car, it would win their respect. It would refresh my dignity. But I have no money, dear Lord. Dear Lord, I need money. Very badly. I am really on my backside."

The old man gazed upon Victor Travesti and the light blue shadows of his eyes darkened.

"You. Ask. *Me*. For. *Money*," he said, his voice faint with incredulity. "You ask *me* for *money*!" As he repeated the question his face began to grow larger, his eyes flashed, and his hands swelled. The old man's face became the face of a radiant beast, huge and furious, blazing.

Victor felt his underpants get wet. He began to weep and dropped his other knee to the floor and clasped his hands together to beg for mercy, but the old man's rage continued to grow. The ceiling lifted above his head to accommodate it, and the walls bulged outward as the waves of fury radiated against them.

"You ask me for *money*!?"

He was on his feet now, bellowing. Victor slipped onto all fours and crawled wildly toward the door, but the old man caught him by the seat of his pants and the scruff of his neck, lifting him with enormous hands, his voice now a wind tunnel of rage, the words no longer distinguishable. Victor was flung against the door, knocking it off its hinges. It toppled, smacked the floor with a hard flat report. Dust rose in small clouds around its edges.

Victor tried to scrabble to his feet, but the old man was on him again, picked him up by his shirt front like a suitcase and chucked him down the stairs. Victor Travesti tumbled, feeling the wooden edges of steps punching his kidney, his ribs, the bones of his cheek. He rolled to a stop against the entry door, which shattered, raining shards of lettered glass upon him. In terror, he looked up the staircase, but the old man did not pursue him. He only stood on the top landing, glaring with enormous eyes of fury down upon the heaped body of Victor Travesti.

Victor crawled out the door, took hold of a fire hydrant and hoisted himself to his feet. His one hand was pulsating. He cradled it in the palm of the other. The middle finger lay at a sharp angle from the middle joint and throbbed painfully. He tucked his shirt into his pants, buttoned the collar at his throat, tried to tuck down the torn flap that hung from his hip pocket.

Cradling his injured hand, he shuffled toward the bus stop, uncertain what to do. He would go home to his mother. She could call Dr. DiAngelo. Dr. DiAngelo would splint Victor's finger. He would drink an espresso and anisette and eat some stella dora bread. He would take a nap and when he woke again, his mother would have baked some zitti for him, and he would be calm.

The carpet men stood in his path.

Victor Travesti drew back, tried to circle around them, but they stepped to the side to block his way again. "Leave me alone," he whimpered. "I broke my finger."

"Oh," said the thick-bellied red-headed one to the quiet, smirking one. "He broke his finger."

"Yeah, gee, poor guinea broke his finger. He wants us to leave him alone."

"Have you no culture?" Victor Travesti inquired icily. "Are you *animali*?"

The red-head cupped a hair-knuckled paw behind his ear. "Come again, Salvatori? You said *what* to me?"

"That is not my name," said Victor Travesti. "Leave me alone. My finger!"

The carpet man reached for the lapels of Victor Travesti's shirt.

"I'll leave you alone," he said. "Come 'ere, Salvatori."

Victor shrieked with indignation and fear as he was dragged down, kicked in the thigh, shoved and stuffed by the two men into a half rolled synthetic Persian carpet. He flailed, was kicked hard in the buttock, the arm; he caught his injured finger, cried out with exquisite pain.

The thick man knelt with one knee on Victor's gut, pinning

him, as the other, snuffling with laughter and excitement, began to roll the carpet. Victor kicked and twisted, and just before the carpet roll closed over his face, he saw, watching from the window above the street, the old man's blazing eyes.

Then the carpet was over his face, was lifted and tossed onto the stack of other carpets in the back of the van. Victor could not move. He felt another carpet tossed on top of his. The air was very close and tight. He could not fill his lungs. He realized — even as he heard the ignorant muffled laughter outside, as he heard the van's rear door smack shut, as he heard the ignition wheeze and catch, and his consciousness slowly began to dim from lack of oxygen — that he was going to die. He realized that he was going to die and that these two carpetmen, when they found his body, would be stricken with terror, would be baptized with a terrible guilt that might change the rest of their lives. All because of their stupidity in not realizing he would die if they did this to him.

It hardly seemed fair. Any of it. He had done nothing to deserve this. Nothing. Perhaps it was stupid of him to have asked for money, but he needed money. Very badly.

His eyelids lowered in the wooly airless darkness, and the tight gasping fury of his lungs stilled, and he knew that he was crossing the border to whatever awaited him — nothing or something, disintegration or the reflection of spirit for a time or forever — as the humming motor of the van faded off into a sleep which slowly ceased to dream him.

FORTUNE, FATE, GOD, KIPLING, ROBERT CRUMB, A BROKEN RADIO, AND THE FATHER OF MY FRIEND WHO TORTURED TURTLES
Commentary on
"What Does God Care About Your Dignity, Victor Travesti?"

"What Does God Care About Your Dignity, Victor Travesti?" came to me in two phases.

In the first phase, riding home from the office on a bus one evening, gazing out the window, I must have observed some untoward behavior on the part of somebody, because a voice of judgement began to speak in my mind: "You were so much greater than the monkies. I had such hopes for you. The monkies were so stupid. All they ever did was fiddle with themselves and giggle and throw their crap at each other. But you! You had advantages. You had capacities never before seen. Then I ask myself what was it all for? You question your motives. Who or what was it for? I admit, I liked the sport. I liked to see them with spears running naked through the forest going after the tigers, shouting my praises..."

I had been nodding. This was almost a dream. I slipped the notepad from my shirt and wrote it down and the voice had the feel to it of a voice that was going to tell me an entire story. When I got home I waited anxiously to finish dinner, to sit on the sofa amidst my family, the kids playing on the floor, my wife reading a book, the television running, and me with a pad on my knee -- my favorite place to write in those days.

I had the sheet from the bus before me, and I tried to get

more life from it, to get it to continue or, backing up, to start at some earlier phase, but there was nothing, nothing. A mere scrap of a voice. Before I went to bed that night I pitched that scrap of paper with the scrap of voice on the heap of similar scraps to one side of the desk in my little work room. The history of such scraps of paper was well known to me. When it got too tall to stay upright without beginning to slide down over the edge of the desk, I would take the bottom-most layer and shove it into a manila envelope which would go into a carton in top of the closet. When that carton at top of the closet was full, it would go down into the ugly room in the basement from which few notes ever found their way out again.

The voice speaking about the monkies — fairly clearly to me the voice of some sort of god, perhaps of God Himself — was now in the scrap pile.

Perhaps a month later, one rainy Saturday, I stood at the bus stop across the submerged highway from our house, waiting for a bus to take me somewhere I no longer can recall. I stood in a raincoat two steps out of the bus shelter, while on the bench beneath the shelter overhang sat two elderly ladies discussing the rain.

"It's sad for all the little boys who wanted to play ball today," one of the ladies said.

Such treacly sentiment seemed to want to bring out the worst in me, the most malicious cynicism. *Let them drown*, I thought.

"And think of all the families who wanted to go on picnics," the other woman said.

Let them eat their grief, thought I, suddenly realizing that this was the voice of a fictional character, sparked off by the sticky-sweet sentiment of these two probably perfectly decent elderly ladies.

Who is speaking? I wondered, without allowing the question even to find words in my mind; the thing was to let that trickle grow to a flow. Then I was on the bus, pad and pen in hand, and the bus — which in fact was driving from the north Copenhagen suburb of Hellerup to Nørreport station, perhaps fifteen minutes away — suddenly was driving in my imagination through my old neighborhood in north Queens, Long Island, moving through the shabby neighborhoods of Corona, Jackson Heights, Woodside, Sunnyside. And observing the passing shabbiness was a man whose name I came to understand was Victor Travesti, a man whose bitterness (LET THEM EAT THEIR GRIEF) I came to understand was the result of the fact that he had been stripped of everything in his life. He was a proud *Calibrese* and his wife had run off with an Irishman. A Jewish judge had awarded his wife and her Irish fornicator custody of Victor's children. In distress, he had lost his business, his car, so that he had to ride on buses. In short, Victor Travesti had been stripped of his dignity, and he was now on his way to visit his sons in the house where his wife slept with the Irish fornicator.

Now I did not know where this journey would actually lead him, I only knew that something was going to happen. On the bus, despite his secret scorn, Victor behaves gallantly to the elderly ladies. He charms them — somewhat hypocritically, in a bid to salvage his injured dignity — and when getting off the bus he pauses to help one of the ladies who has been thrown off balance, this moment's delay decides the fate of the remainder of his life.

I did not know that this would be the case other than that one of the old ladies, attempting to flirt with Victor, mentions that her astrology column today had said she would meet a tall, dark stranger. The old lady was hinting to me in this way that some fateful event was about to occur.

And what can be more fateful than being shit on by a bird? Supposedly, this — like stepping in dog dirt — should signal good fortune, but immediately I could see this would be a reversal of that tradition. In Victor's world, getting shit on is nothing more nor less than getting shit on. My suspicion was confirmed when suddenly two thug-like men standing in front of a truck laugh at

Victor's misfortune. These men, I realized, were straight from hell and come to take Victor off with them and when I saw what was written on the side of their truck — KIPLING KARPET KO. — I quickly, as in the light of a flare, intuited a great deal more about my story which I labored not to allow myself to KNOW, lest it be lost in the light. (Perhaps I might also mention here that when one of the carpet men points at Victor in his distress and says, "I want to sing like the boidies do, tweet tweet tweet," this is a kind of tribute to R. Crumb, one of his "Pete the Plumber" stories from Hytone Comix, in which a plumber is accidentally flushed down the toilet and ends up in a kind of *salle d'attente* amidst the pipes where people covered in shit engage in philosophical debate until finally the plumber escapes and out in the fresh air marches down the middle of the avenue singing, "I want to sing like the boidies do..." I have always found Crumb an artist of the unconscious and as you will see when, if, you read on, the idea of the plumber is not foreign to where this story was leading me either.)

Victor's reaction to his misfortune is, of course, in keeping with his character — Victor's fate is never in his stars, but in his character. His character has led him to where he is, and it is his character which continues him along the way.

He evades the thugs, puts his jacket and tie in the cleaners for a quick rinsing because his dignity will not allow him to appear to his wife and her Irish fornicator in disarray. As he agrees to return to the cleaners in an hour, the black man working the presser pulls it down with a blast of steam, and I realized that Victor was still continuing on his path to hell. (This black presser was, in fact, a figure from my youth, a man who worked for a local dry cleaners called, no stuff, Fortune Dry Cleaner, in Jackson Heights, just down from the shoe shop where I worked afternoons throughout highschool. I can remember the tall, mysterious black man drawing down the lid of that presser, the steam hissing hellishly up around him, though I did not know at that time that I wanted to be a writer or that this figure would appear years later in a story about Victor Travesti at the gates of hell. In fact, I did not quite know until this moment, writing this essay, that that was where the black presser came from.)

Leaving the dry cleaners, Victor takes a walk to kill time and sees an upstairs shop which has a sign on the door advertising a gypsy fortune teller, Esther. This shop, in fact, was occupied by fortune tellers in my neighborhood when I was growing up (at the other end of the block from Fortune Dry Cleaners — how amazing sometimes is the symmetry of the physical world which presents itself to us) and I had always wanted to visit there, but was too young, hadn't the money, and was afraid to. Now I would get my chance.

Continuing to follow fate and fortune, Victor climbs the stairs and finds, of course, three doors. There are always three doors. But two of them are locked — there is only one path for Victor; he goes through the third door.

Here to my great surprise I saw a figure from my past. The father of an old friend with whom I had grown up. This man, a plumber by profession, was a very kind man who had been enormously generous to all his son's friends. He used to drive us to the beach, buy us malteds and burgers, take us to ball games. He lived with his family in a very modest apartment although he made a good living, was more interested in enjoying life than amassing material goods. He was full of laughter and affection and just about one of the nicest adults I knew when I was a boy.

His son, too, had seemed a very nice fellow but as we grew into puberty, I began to notice some unpleasant traits in him. One day, he told me with great merriment and excitement how he had bought a bunch of heavy duty fireworks, cherry bombs and ashcans, and had used them to detonate a box turtle he had found in the woods, had blown the creature up again and again until its shell was smashed and its body destroyed and it died, but slowly. It was not so much that I couldn't understand that he could do such a thing, but I could not comprehend how he could have told the tale with such merriment, so utterly oblivious to what a nasty, sadistic act he had performed.

Years later, when we were both in our twenties, I met him again and he invited me home with him. He was single, still living in his parents' apartment. His mother was dead, and his father, who had been considerably older than she, was now in his late seventies and clearly somewhat senile. He was sitting in the apartment in a chair wearing a plaid flannel shirt and a mustard-colored necktie. I was delighted to see him, but his son interrupted as I tried to talk to his father.

"He's all fucked up, don't talk to him, forget him, have a drink." To his father, he said, "Shut up and leave us the fuck alone," then sniggered as he poured me a drink as though I might be amused. As we sat and talked and drank our drink, I glanced at his father, clearly distressed and unhappy and hurt sitting on his straightback chair, his tie up to his throat, though possessing a certain dignity. My ex-friend told me that he had taken over his father's plumbing business. Without shame or guile, he told me about how he had made a science of bilking old ladies who called him to look at a leaky toilet. He would tell them the toilet needed replacement, quote them a price, would replace the toilet with a second hand one, offer to remove the old "defective" one, then proceed to sell it to the next old lady who phoned him with a leaky toilet. Hard to believe my old friend, with whom I had shared so many pleasant summer days as a lad, could have turned out so baldly malicious. Even harder to believe that his poor father, who had been such a kind, spiritual, non-materialistic man, should end his days — having given his son everything, as far as I could see — being mistreated by the son, abused. The image of the father sitting in that chair so hurt yet somehow so dignified remained with me for years.

Approximately seventeen years later, I saw the man again in a sense — this time he was sitting behind the door which Victor Travesti opened, thinking that he was about to enter Esther's fortune parlor. There he sat, my friend's father, in the rubble of a bombed out room — the bombed out room of the past perhaps?

One of the details in that room, which came to me without thought, was "a gutted yellow plastic radio with a crack in the casing." This is an autobiographical detail; for my eleventh birthday I asked everyone to give me money instead of presents because there was something I wanted to buy. Somehow I received the lordly sum of thirty-six dollars, more money than I had ever had in my life, and I went out and bought a Motorola clock radio in a yellow plastic casing that looked like the dashboard of a Buick Special. That was the year I associated with my friend, the plumber's son, and in fact that radio wound up cracked and discarded like all the heap of broken things of the past. Now I realize this detail can mean little to anyone other than myself, but I left it in the story because it seemed to me to fit metaphorically as well as physically: a broken radio, smashed communication, plastic, cracked... The image gave the sense of something I wanted in there — that it also has private meaning to me is irrelevant. All our favorite, cherished stories, I would swear, abound with such details.

In any event, I was surprised to see my friend's father there sitting in the chair, and even more surprised when he opened his mouth and began to say, "You were so much greater than the monkies. I had such hopes for you..." (I hurried in to retrieve that scrap of paper I had written on the bus a month or so before and cast onto the heap of discarded notes.)

Then I realized that my friend's father was an image of a benevolent god who had attempted to create a wonderful Eden for mankind, a fallible god perhaps, for surely something must have transpired to sour my friend so. In fact, I can recall that we used to pick on him some because he was a somewhat gullible, naive kid — perhaps his father had taught him only kindness without giving him the capacity for brutality people need to be able to call upon occasionally to survive in this harsh world. Perhaps god had made some mistakes. Perhaps god wished to discuss this with someone. Perhaps god had engineered a meeting with Victor Travesti to discuss this matter — a more kindly god than the one of the Job story. This one is not conversing with the devil, this one wants to level with the man himself instead. This god is looking for help; he has given man the power to think, to consider, to weigh, and he is looking for this man to level with him, too, rather than to ask, as the Lord asks Job, "where were you when I created the universe?"

By this point the story was running on its own steam. All I had to do was not to force it, to let it have its lead, to follow its headlights through the dark and to observe, while writing, to witness as I wrote the report, as the facts of the situation slowly dawned on the not exceedingly bright Victor Travesti. In time, he comes to realize that he is indeed in the presence of God, that perhaps all the events of his life, every moment of every day had led him to this ultimate experience of being in the presence of the creator.

Here again, we see — I saw — Victor chosen for a fate he could in no way rise to. Think of the wonderful multitude of possibilities offered by a conversation with a god willing to talk, a god willing to level with you, a god willing even to admit to fallibility.

Victor knows the right gestures — he kneels, though not before dusting the floor to avoid soiling his pants (dignity in what he wears), and then he pops the question foremost in his heart: he asks for money. Not wisdom, enlightenment, forbearance, but money.

Now I did not know that Victor would do this until he did, and I confess that I laughed when I heard him say it because I knew that the carpet men were waiting downstairs for him, I knew that this was inevitable, but I did not yet know there was one last twist remaining in the fate of Victor — whom, I must admit, I had come to like somewhat, despite his shortcomings. It was really not a great deal he asked for — just a little bit of dignity. Unfortunately, he steadfastly declined to examine what dignity might be. And his unexamined life was not worth living, as Plato's Socrates said.

Whatever, this god in the garb of a senile plumber is still god, still full of the Old Testament, still capable of rage, and he is, after all, a god. Slighted, he explodes, rages, picks Victor up like a piece of luggage and pitches him down the stairs right into the clutches of the Kipling Karpet Ko people.

Now I knew as soon as they appeared what they were going to do but I did not allow myself to become aware of it until after it happened. The combination of the words Kipling and Karpet related to a story I had once read by Rudyard Kipling about some British officers somewhere or other, India no doubt, who had dealt with someone they disapproved of by getting him drunk, rolling him in a carpet and pitching the carpet in a train or a van or some such to be transported off into the middle of nowhere. It occurred to me when I read the conclusion — which seemed to want to be taken as good old chap jovial British stuff — that that man would suffocate, that those officers were murderers. And I knew that this was the final fate awaiting Victor.

As he submits unwillingly to it, he looks up and sees the blue eyes of god staring out the upstairs window at him, unrelenting, unmerciful. Then the carpet is over his face and he realizes that he is going to die, he realizes that these men who have rolled him in the carpet did not realize that they are killing him, that when they discover his dead body, their lives will be utterly changed, baptized by the knowledge of their misdeed (for they are not only hounds from hell, they are also human beings — or at least fictional shades of human beings.)

And thus, I discovered, in the very last part of the story that Victor could never have lived any other way, but that in death, in his dying, he achieves a moment of some dignity, expands beyond the limits that held him in life and is, thus, somehow chastened. In some way perhaps his death is his savlation — as suggested by the mocking name the carpetman gives him, Salvatori.

There remained only to put a title on it. I knew it was a story about dignity and god and god's indifference to the material dignity of man, and there was a title to a story by Harold Jaffe which I had read several years before and which suggested itself in the first page when Victor thinks, LET THEM EAT THEIR GRIEF. The Jaffe story was titled, "Eat Your Grief, Cora Dance." I admired that title and hoped to have a title something like that for myself some day, so all these elements came together in "What Does God Care About Your Dignity, Victor Travesti?"

I finished the story and re-read it and thought, Who the hell is ever going to want to read that?! But, to my pleasant surprise, it was taken by *New Letters* the first time out (and opened a connection for me with that fine journal which has been one of my major encouragements over the past ten years and more) and has been reprinted several times since.

My object in wanting to tell about how this story was written is to give interested readers a glimpse into the intuitive manner in which some stories are written and to give writers still at an early stage of struggling with their craft encouragement to listen to themselves.

DUST

Infinitesimal monsters people the dust. That was what she told him. Tiny grey creatures with claws that affix themselves inside your nose and other organs. She had seen photographs of them. Millions of them in every clump of dust. Billions beneath a bed, across the surface of a shelf, in the books, curtains, rising in motes of sunlight from the floor. That was what she stared at so intently on the wood plank floor: two fluffs of dust nestled in the angle to the wall.

Volk sat on the windowsill and watched her, long bright yellow hair swept back from her face in a hand delicate as china, slender body impeccable in skintight black denims, slim shoulders in a scoopneck sweater, high cheekbones, pale eyes, fine lips. He glanced out the window to the street below, where a blue Mustang sat gathering snow, a '75 convertible. Volk had had one just like it the summer of that year, and an uncomplicated girlfriend named Evelyn Cruz who had dimples and a gorgeous butt. Evelyn. Whatever happened to sweet simple Evelyn?

Snow fell steadily in big soft flakes down the darkening sky, while Cathleen stared at the two dust clumps, moaned with disgust as she bent her knees to dip closer, her hair swept protectively behind her. She feared getting dust in her hair. And plant lice. And worst of all, she feared The Big A, a disease she kept attempting to bribe physicians to assure her she suffered from. She would not even call it by its name. **A**, she called it.

"Cathleen, I am sorry to say it, but you need help. You are not well. In your thoughts."

She crouched forward, bent at the waist, crescent eyes blazing at him. "*Nasty!*" she whispered hoarsely. Gave him gooseflesh. "*You,*" she whispered. "You're the sick one. *You* make me unwell."

At the bar in Scanlon's, above the rumbling subway, Volk nursed a beer and called upon the cold German elements of his blood to protect him from pity, which threatened to send him off the edge. If there were an edge. Perhaps he had no edge at all. Just ice. That Kraut blood. French Kraut. Worse kind. Cold pride. His German name hid the fact his mother had been Irish, his father half-Irish. His father's father's family the only survivors. Tall cranky Alsatian types who lived into their eighties. Let me be one of them. Deliver me from the Irish Catholic tragedy. Let me pack my bag and leave her and not give it another thought. Tell it as a memory one day: Poor girl was sick in the head. No choice but to leave her.

He could stay with his cousin Beth until he found a new place. But the thought of his cousin Beth Clancy in her little overheated house with all the windows shut tight and her traipsing around in bathrobe and slippers terrified him. Smother there. In the heat, the dust, the silence, the doing of nothing, the passive shaking of the head and the doing of nothing.

And what would happen to Cathleen? She was already out of a job. You can't just stay home for a week without calling in and expect to come back. *Sorry, I couldn't call in, but you see the phone had dust all over it.*

No job, no pay. No pay, no rent. No rent, no apartment. Then what? Out with the homeless. Pack up your plastic bags and take it on the arches.

She had no one, just her brother, and there was no help to find from him. Volk tried, hoping to interest Walter in taking over the problem. But Walter was convinced his sister was faking, as, he said, she had always done all her life. And anyway, Walter did not believe in psychiatry. *It's them that are crazy. She doesn't need psychiatry, she needs philosophy. She needs spunk! Guts!* And in any event, his money was all tied up in real estate. And finally, he had no room in his life for such a liability of a human being at this time, as he was currently negotiating his engagement to marry Mrs. Maxwell T. Farrell, widow of the prominent novelist. He could not allow his sister's playacting at madness to upset the lady he adored or his prospects of contracting exclusive rights to adore her for the rest of their lives.

Volk looked around Walter's living room, speculating how to get the man to offer him a drink. It was a Tudor City suite. Bare walls, overstuffed chairs, dark. Very Irish. "Will you take her name when you marry her, Walter?" Volk asked.

"More and more do just that every day," the tall, slender, tow-headed man said, looking up from the book in his lap.

"You could call yourself Mr.Mrs. Maxwell T. Farrell."

"I don't know." Walter's mouth was a tortured oval of anxiety. He was seated beside his *Great Books of the Western World* bookcase, Clifton Fadiman's *Lifetime Reading Plan* open in his lap. He was up to Aristotle so far, only 2,500 years of literature left to cover in the decades remaining him.

"Did you know Aristotle has been dropped from the new edition of the *Great Books*?" Volk asked.

The tortured oval mouth focused on him. "Not a chance, Vance. They dropped Fielding. They dropped Sterne. They are *considering* dropping Darwin. But they will *never, ever* drop Aristotle. No true classical liberal arts education could be without Aristotle."

"Darwin? You're kidding me, right? They're dropping Darwin?"

"Mortimer Adler has his reasons."

"Yeah. Fear of fundamentalists." Volk noticed a row of crystal goblets in the china cabinet. He stooped, admiring them. "These are nice," he said. "Very attractive. Be nice to drink a beer from one of these beauties."

"Not a drop in the house," said Walter. "Actually, I am

studying just now by the way."

Volk gazed down at the man, seated in a plush chair, wearing leather slippers, a cashmere sweater. He considered punching him. Quick right hook to his pointed beak. Spray blood across the pages of the *Poetics*.

"If you won't help her, Walter, who will?"

"Why no one I hope and trust. She needs to learn to help herself."

"You *bastard*."

"My mother and my father were quite my own, thank you."

The bartender at Scanlon's looked more like a corpse than a mortician, Volk decided. Volk had always thought he looked like a mortician, but now actually he could see the man looked dead, like a dead man on his feet. Volk read somewhere that the average family size of American morticians was double the national average for all other professions. Horny types. He noticed this one always had his eye on Cathleen's hair when they came in together. *It's a fine head of hair you have on you, girl!* he said to her once, spontaneous ejaculation from the grey lips. What was his name? Kelly. Right. Another Irish. Maybe Kelly would care for the girl? Sit there, brush her hair for her. Hundred strokes a night.

Volk wondered what Cathleen was doing up in her apartment just now. Tweezing dust clumps into jars with screw-on lids. She had a shelf of them in the kitchen cupboard which she planned to send out for testing. Or perhaps she was hanging the mattresses out the window again to freeze the plant lice she was convinced migrated from the little potted elderberry she gave a Vikings' funeral down the incinerator chute. Then of course she had to sleep on the floor lest the heat of her body defrost them. And, sleeping on the floor, she risked the dust monsters, so she didn't sleep at all but squatted on the dining table with a pot of coffee wearing nothing but her underpants, looking, he had to admit, quite cute if you didn't know she was mad. Or perhaps she was spraying Lysol into the motor of the refrigerator which the dust monsters were particularly attracted to. The humming, she said, soothed them.

Volk signalled, watched the dour-faced Kelly approach the taps to refill his mug, watched the freckled, redheaded girl with the underslung jaw and a white apron wrapped about her hips washing glasses in the stainless steel sink. She looked so uncomplicated and fresh-faced. It filled him with nostalgia for simpler times, simpler ways.

Kelly thumped a foaming mug on the bar before Volk, who asked, "Who's the red-head?"

Kelly's flat brown eyes, his grey sagging face focused on Volk. Then, "Sheila?" he called with his parched voice.

She looked up, smiling, from the sink. "Yes, Dad?"

Outside, snow was falling lightly down the dark Manhattan afternoon. Volk walked hunched in his thin-soled shoes, hands in his pockets. She is not my responsibility. It is not my fault her mind is tortured, that she will end in a state mental hospital with drooling maniacs, subjected to shock treatments, drug fogs, medicated into twilight. I can do nothing about it. I'm not her husband.

He reached their building, looked through the glass door to where the half-deaf Australian doorman sat on a straightback chair holding one of his oxblood shoes in both hands. Volk thought about her up there, skinny and frightened, turned his back and retraced his steps through the snow to Scanlon's where he resumed his place at the bar, fingering his mug. He sipped, thought about his life, the entirety of it, all the dead, all the gone events, the jobs that came to nothing, the futile plans, wishes. I am *not* nobody.

Why? He thought about his ancestor, Frederich Volk, who fled Baden Baden in 1869 at the age of 16 to avoid conscription in the Franco-Prussian Wars, fled with his fiancé Viola Beauzart of Strasbourg. Volk had a photo of old Fred Volk in Brooklyn, 13 years later, in suit and hat, thumbs in his vest pockets, smiling, 29 years old, author of the chain of events that would lead, inexorably, to this moment.

He thought about that day, six months before, at Yesterday's when he sat over a late morning capuccino reading the *Times* classified and suddenly, standing over him, smiling, holding her hair back with her delicate china fingers, was a beautiful woman. She twinkled at him, said, "I like your face."

They drank New York State champagne and had a lovely afternoon, walked in the summer night all the way up to her apartment in Germantown while Volk played "Amazing Grace" on a toilet-paper comb kazoo.

At the pay phone beside the front window, Volk riffled through the yellow pages to *psychiatrist...* He ran his finger down the columns, looking not at names, but addresses, found what he wanted, dialed, and watched the snow fall while the number rang in his ear.

Dr. Saltine was small, a head shorter than Volk, who was himself not tall. The doctor sat in a wooden armchair on the opposite edge of an egg-shaped, cobalt blue carpet, watching Volk without speaking. He wore a pencil moustache and his eyes bulged slightly and were lopsided. He sat up very straight on the edge of the chair.

Volk said, "Are you an Adlerian?"

The doctor sighed. "Tell me in which way I may help you."

"Well," Volk said, "It's not me actually, but a friend, my girlfriend actually. I mean, I guess that sounds funny. Like the classic disclaimer. Hey, doc, it's not me that needs help, it's my friend."

The lopsided eyes registered nothing, only stared at him. "May I ask you something?" Volk asked.

"Of course."

"How much does this cost exactly?"

The doctor sighed again. "Let *me* ask *you* a question, Mr. Volk. How did you happen to come to *me*? Why *me*?"

"Well, I liked your address. I wouldn't feel obliged to escort her here every time she came. It's *safe*."

"That is not the most suitable criterion upon which to choose your analyst."

"Not mine. My friend's."

"Indeed. But I can refer you to a clinic that you will be able to afford."

"Who said I couldn't afford it? All I asked was how much it cost?"

"If you have to ask, Mr. Volk, it is too expensive."

This, then, is how misfortune comes. In the guise of happiness. "Why me?" he asked Cathleen. "Why did you come up to me at Yesterday's that time?"

"Cause I liked your face."

They were sharing a rare moment of lucidity, dust forgotten, plant lice out of mind, all the glass jars bombed down the incinerator shaft, The Big A unmentioned for a week. They made love on the big bed in the little bedroom, sad New York snowlight at the window, illuminating the white walls of the darkened room. Volk held her. He couldn't quite get it up. Her fragile body in his arms, he gazed at the blue grey window and considered the fact that she was the only person in the universe he was in any way attached to anymore, and the attachment was such a very short one. Why me? Cause she liked my face.

A beautiful woman likes your face, approaches you in a bar where you sit out of work, about to lose your apartment, out of friends, and you think to yourself she is some wild Swede who loves you on first sight, and all manner of things now will be well. Cool uptown nights of passion, cool blue Scandinavian eyes.

Now she buried her face into the center of his chest and began to sniffle. "How could I?" she whispered. "How could I do this to you?"

He smoothed her hair. "There, there," he said. "Do what?"

"Expose you to such a disease like that."

189

Dour-faced Kelly placed a foaming mug of beer on the bar before Volk. "How is the Mrs.?" he asked.

"Getting a crewcut."

"Such a *fine* head of hair she has."

Volk dropped a coin in the juke box, punched buttons, heard B. B. King croon,

I'm goin to Chicago, baby
Sorry I can't take you,
Cause they ain't no room in Chicago,
Fo a monkey-face woman like you.

Actually Cathleen cut her own hair. With a kitchen shears. The golden clippings were in a screwtop jar in the cupboard.

And in the clinic recommended by Dr. Saltine, Volk told an enormously corpulent woman all about his lady friend and asked, "Can you help me?"

"Yes," she said.

"Yes?"

"Yes, I can help you," she said. "If you truly *want* to be helped."

"Dr. Saltine told me it wouldn't cost so much here."

"If the treatment is cheap, you won't value it, Mr. Volk."

"Well, about how much would it have to cost for me to value it?"

"In special cases of need, for qualified individuals, we take the minimum fee only. Which is one hundred dollars per session. I will want you to come twice a week for the first few months."

"Well it's not me," Volk said. "It's my friend, a lady friend. It's really quite tragic."

"That is why I will want you to come twice a week at first. I will need many hours with you. Tell me about your mother."

"My mother? Why do you mention my mother?"

"Does the thought of your mother upset you?"

Volk looked across the desk at the woman, at her thick lips, her large, smooth-skinned face; her arms in a sleeveless dress made him think of the Christmas ham he would have to scrounge up the money for soon. He wondered what her age might be, involuntarily pictured her naked, found himself excited, shook his head to be free of the sensation.

"What are you thinking about right now, Mr. Volk?"

"My mother. My poor dead mother. She was, in fact, a tragic case."

"Exactly. Don't you begin to see the pattern? You say your lady friend is tragic. Your mother was tragic. A man always marries his mother, Mr. Volk."

"My mother wasn't my type, Doctor."

"Oh, they never are, Mr. Volk."

Volk came home to find Cathleen squatting in her yellow underpants on the dining table, her hair a ragged mat clipped an inch from her skull. On the floor by the door was an enormous black plastic bag of laundry. Every cotton garment and sheet in the house. The plant lice and dust monsters were partial to cotton, especially white cotton. It all needed to be washed on a program where the water was at least sixty degrees centigrade. It was the only way. If you put them in the freezer, they could go dormant. The only way to kill them was with heat, boiling heat.

Volk felt like Santa Claus, hiking the streets with the huge bag over his shoulder, along the slushy sidewalks, winter barren trees festooned with delicate Christmas lights, past shop windows where mechanical Santas nodded and laughed slowly, elves at their feet hammering and grinning. The sidewalk was an inch of slush through which he scuffled with his thin leather shoes, weaving through the crowd of shoppers, considering the fact that Cathleen's madness might be a reflection of his own.

Was that a possibility? Or did the lady shrink only mean he was with Cathleen because she was mad, because he sought out mad women? He had not told her about his mother, not specifically, not about how she looked on her bed with all her own mother's jewelry displayed on her breast, her hands crossed, face white, the white of death. Volk found her there like that, touched her hand, and his fingers flew away as from an electric shock. The touch of death was uglier than pain.

In the laundromat, two women in curlers watched Volk out of the corners of their eyes as he loaded up three machines, dug into his pockets for coins, fed dollar bills into the changer. The coins rattled into the slot, then the room was silent but for the hum of dryers and slosh of washers, the hushed conversation of the two women who sat at the far end of the room from him, sorting laundry, talking.

Volk sat on a bench at the front window and read *The Post* while snowflakes slashed down outside and melted on the pavement. The news of the day was that a New Jersey woman had been awarded damages from a nightclub where a male stripper, swinging across the stage in a Tarzan outfit, had fallen on her, causing her grievous mental anguish and loss of earnings; a reporter was seeking the source of a story that a cactus purchased in a discount chain store had contained dozens of tarantula eggs which hatched during the night and escaped into the city; a crack dealer named Bruno Fat Cat da Silva had been arrested for having his wife murdered because she stole from him and "spent it on a dude"; Miss USA had captured the coveted Miss World crown; the city welfare rolls had hit a new high, and a privately owned, but very cherished horse which had been lost in the Grand Canyon had been lifted out on a rope by helicopter after a two-week "night-mare."

Volk folded the paper and laid it on the bench, stared out at the snow and the people moving in thick strands along the street. He could hear the faint sound of car horns from the avenue.

It was warm in the laundromat. It seemed a charmed niche away from all the troubles of his life, of the city. The hollow drumming of the dryer calmed him. He leaned back, breathed slowly, wished he could sit here like this forever, noticed a bulletin board on the wall between the soap and cigarette machines, stood, went to it, idly browsed among the hand-lettered offers of babysitting, second hand TVs, bicycles, discount travel, economy moving services. One card caught him, a printed card with an odd double-pronged logo over the words:

TO KNOW, TO DARE, TO WILL,
TO KEEP SILENCE: YOU CAN!

Printed beneath was the name Eliphas Crowley and a telephone number.

At the appointed door of a dark narrow building on 21st Street, Volk rang the bell and, as instructed, spoke the word, "Sarax," into the intercom. The door popped open. In the tiny lobby, nothing happened for several minutes, during which Volk felt he was watched. Then the inner door too popped open, and he entered a small, doorless room. There was no place to go from there, no place to sit, no windows, bare walls, a single light overhead. Then he noticed a picture on the far wall, an old black and white photographic portrait of a heavy-faced bearded man staring straight forward. Volk stepped closer. The eyes were so alive! They moved. Volk gasped, a panel in the wall popped open, and the man in the picture stood before him, staring intently at him, wearing a blue robe with a gold rope belt.

The man was short and stout, and his eyes took liberties which stoked Volk's indignation. He opened his mouth but before he could speak, the little man said, "To prevent a person from firing a pistol in your face while you are looking in the barrel, say *Pax Sax Sarax.* To cure a toothache, say *Arigdem Margidem, Sturgidem* seven times on a Tuesday or Thursday, providing the moon is waning. To heal a fractured bone, chant *Motas vareta daries,* then splint the bone with a green reed, and say, *Dardares Astatories dissunapita.* To cure an ailing cow write the following words on an egg — *Curiat Suriat Marut Murat* — and give it to the affected animal to eat. These words have no meaning, but are impressive upon dark spirits."

Volk said, "I'm sorry. This is absurd."

Crowley laughed. "Of course it is! That is half the power.

And believe me, it is no coincidence you came to me today. Just the darkest time of the year. The time of the Saturnalia. Now step in and tell me about the woman."

Inside they sat at a fireplace, and Volk said, "What makes you think it is a woman?"

Crowley was staring at him again. He said, "Everything rests upon the principle of the stimulation of the inert yet all-potential *Binah*."

"*Binah?*"

"Yes. By the dynamic *Hukmak*. You are the *hukmak*. She is the *Binah*. She is understanding, you are wisdom. She is female, you are male. She is number 3, you are number 2."

To avoid Crowley's black gaze, Volk looked at the wall above the mantle, saw a framed wood print of a woman churning butter. He stared at the picture, closed one eye, thought suddenly it looked like a woman with a long nose straddling a broomstick. He looked back to Crowley.

"So the number 2 has to stimulate the number 3 then?"

"Precisely."

"Is that, uh, expensive?"

"It costs, my friend, nothing less than everything. But first things first. Empty your pockets and I'll give you a Gypsy blessing."

In Scanlon's at the Subway, Volk drank Justification Brews and did the Preservation Shuffle with Kelly's redheaded daughter with her calming underslung jaw and simple smile, while Kelly *père* looked on gravely. The bar room was decorated with plastic holly and mistletoe. Volk, who was thinking about the fact that he was coveting a man's daughter in the presence of the man, put his hands on his hips and twisted his back to the music, looked into Sheila Kelly's blue eyes, and said,

"Ale, man, ale's the stuff to drink
For fellows whom it hurts to think!"

He stole a glance at her father, who was polishing the bar,

shuffling along the wood skids. The music ended. Sheila laughed and hugged him with her arms and shoulders, keeping her body free of the embrace, and Volk returned to the bar, said, "Your Sheila is a darling, Jack Kelly!"

"You'll have my license," Kelly said.

Volk weaved, trying to interpret the words, then realized he was referring to the establishment's alcohol license, noted the *No Dancing* sign above the cash register.

Kelly refilled Volk's mug and pushed back his money, tapped the bar with his knuckles. Sheila returned from the little girl's room and took her post behind the bar near Volk. A sign. "So, say me some more poetry, Freddy," she said to Volk just as a record dropped into place on the juke box. B. B. King:

> *Ain't no room in Chicago, baby,*
> *Fo a monkey face woman like you.*

Sheila laughed, drew on her Newport, watched Volk with dancing eyes. Volk said, "My ancestor knew how to run. Old Fred Volk knew how to run."

"Is that a poem?" Sheila asked, and Volk melted in the clear blue invitation of her eyes. He leaned closer, whispered, "Dust on an old man's sleeve is all the ash the burnt roses leave." She sighed sweetly. He said, "Pax Sax Sarax: I put a spell on you. You are now in my power."

"Already was," she said and looked up from under her lashes at him, and Volk felt complications arising. He swallowed beer, trying to analyze details, the hug, the gaze, the way she was leaning across the bar showing a hint of her beauties above the neckline of her red and green Christmas blouse, while Papa Kelly shuffled like death along the skids.

Volk headed for the Gents to think, stood at the porcelain with his eyes closed, smiling with ecstasy, heard himself whisper, "A seat on a bus is cheaper than a headshrinker's couch." He shook, zipped, looked into the mirror and saw the face of a full-grown man. He remembered his father once saying, "Old men should not weep. It is insufferable," as silent tears rolled down his

195

scarred boozy cheeks, and Volk felt the ice running through his own heart and the panic filling his gut for all the loss of all the years of his past.

Outside, Sheila stood alone at the juke box. Volk started across the room to her, but stopped halfway across the floor, noting how big, how very big and lumpy she looked from behind and looking at her that way made him feel cheap, made him feel like he was already finding a reason to leave her. The booze soured in his blood. She punched some buttons on the juke, and the Beeb came on singing about Chicago as Volk slipped out into the chill night. He stood swaying in the icy air, thinking about what he would have to take with him to Oregon. He had a buddy there. He could ride the dog to Portland, stay with his buddy, start a new life, another new life. A man is never too old to start another new life. All he needed was his underwear, a clean shirt, a cardboard suitcase, his credit cards.

A sprig of holly hung on the apartment door beneath the peephole and he stared at Cathleen's name there on a white tag, remembering the first time he'd seen this door, when the two of them had walked arm-in-arm all the way uptown from Yesterday's and she recited Millay: "We were very tired and we were very merry/We rode back and forth all night on the Staten Island Ferry...."

Inside, a half-decorated, lopsided dwarf Christmas tree stood on an end table surrounded by an assortment of boxes, colored glass balls nestled in tissue wrapping, a cardboard tray of tinsel, a spray can of artificial snow. On the floor, the vacuum cleaner stood ready for use, hose mounted with a long-snouted attachment for cleaning nooks and crannies. At the base of the tree were two gift boxes. He read the tags. *To Freddy, Love Cathleen.* Both of them. He could hear the sound of the shower from within.

In the bedroom, he fumbled in the back of his sock drawer for his credit cards, passport, Social Security card, all the papers he did not dare carry on his person in the city for fear a mugger would steal his identity. He lifted the cardboard suitcase down from the top of the mildew smelling closet, shoved in his underwear, socks, shirt, a pair of jeans, Louis Untermeyer's *Treasury of Favorite Poems*, a collection of stories by Donald Barthelme. On the back of an unopened letter from Con Edison, he wrote in blue ink, *Dear Cathy, I'm leaving you. Please be happy. Love, Fred.* He balanced the envelope on the tank of the vacuum cleaner, stood staring at the little half-decorated tree on the table.

The shower stopped. Go! He thought. Go! She stood in the doorway of the misted bathroom wearing a blue terry cloth robe, her choppy hair slick wet against her skull, cheeks glowing. Volk watched her delicate fingers unknot the belt, open the robe. "Goodbye," she whispered. "Goodbye and good luck," as the suitcase dropped from his hand and he crossed the carpet to her, saw, over her shoulder, a mote of moonlight at the window, across the little twisted tree, and he whispered into her warm nuzzling ear,

"Dust in the air suspended
Marks the place where the story ended."

ELEMENTS OF "DUST"

One evening when I was about twenty-two years old standing at a bar in my hometown, someone called to me from the shadowy tables at back. It was a young woman, a beautiful young woman, tall and slender, with long straight blond hair and blue eyes and a flashing smile. I asked why she had called to me, and she said, "Because I liked your face." We got to talking, quoted poetry to one another, went home together. Talk about luck!

It turned out that she was convinced she had syphilis, which she referred to as 'S', which for the purpose of my story I updated to 'A'. Her father was, I surmised, a wealthy miser who feared plant lice and once hung all the mattresses in the house out the window because he was convinced they were infested with plant lice. He would not pay for psychiatric help for her, just as he had refused to pay the medical bills of his wife years before — he had loaned her the money and now she was working as a cleaning lady to pay it back.

This girl also had a brother who owned a set of the *Great Books of the Western World*, housed in their own special bookcase, and he planned to read them from start to finish. He was a right wing intellectual and he refused to believe that his sister needed psychiatric help. He also had a penchant for getting involved, when he was in his 20s, with older women who were the widows of prominent men.

I once saw a many-times enlarged photograph of a dust mite and was horrified by it and once read that there are tiny dust-mite-like organisms that live between our eyelashes, and I was so terrified by this information that it seemed to give me a flash insight into madness, how someone could go mad thinking about such things. I also once read somewhere that cockroaches like to nestle in the motor of a refrigerator because the humming soothes them, a fact which seemed quite mad as well.

One of my ancestors was named Frederick Volk, and he did flee Baden Baden in 1869 at the age of sixteen to avoid being conscripted into the German army to fight in the Franco-Prussian wars, and I was acutely aware of the magnificent short story, "Boul de Suif," Maupassant had created in the setting of that year and that place. It always seemed curious to me that part of my family's origin in the U.S. was due to that act of draft dodging — of flight and desertion.

Part of my family was Irish and part was French-German, and the Irish in general seemed to me sometimes morbidly obsessed with sentimental matters ("Death is a luxury we cannot now afford," etc.), while the Alsatian ones seemed cool and aloof and self-possessed.

Now we enter into the basis of the story — a man torn between two halves of a fragmented nature - sentimental and cool — and trapped in a love affair with a hopelessly deranged woman for whom he feels responsible. Which side of him will prevail? The cool side that will allow him to escape and perhaps suffer later the agonies of regret of his sentimental heart? Or the sentimental side which may require him to sacrifice his life to this doomed affair, this poor, tortured girl?

The story, however, began without my knowing anything of what it was about. It began with a sentence: "Infinistesimal monsters people the dust." The first paragraph wrote itself, leading me to see that it was about a character who resembled the girl I had known and about a man who was a drifter with no place to go in life, living in her apartment and watching her go mad.

Having finished the first scene of about a page and a half, I had no idea where I was going. So I went to a bar — that is I let Volk go to a bar of the imagination to think things over. It turned out to be a bar that I once actually visited with the girl in question, a bar called Scanlon's Railway Inn which used to be in Elmhurst, New York, at the foot of the stairs of the now defunct Elmhurst Station of the Long Island Railroad. In the story, the bar is placed by the subway station since I had to transplant it to Manhattan and I liked the idea of its sitting above the rumbling underground. The proprieter was Mr. Scanlon, a kind but sorrowful-faced man who tended the bar and had in fact once said to the girl in queston, "It is a fine head of hair you have on you, girl!"

And the memory of that statement began to suggest a structure for the story, a set of rhyming elements and episodes. Now Mr. Scanlon did have a daugther, whose name and nature escape me except that I seem to remember her as shy and sweet and who did have a fine head of red hair and who was nothing like the daughter in this story. That daughter, Sheila, is pure fiction and named for the Celtic fertility goddess Sheela na gig, though I did not think of that when it came to me. The line, "Say me some poetry," which gave me a glimpse into Sheila's person, is a line spoken to me in real life fifteen years ago in Paris by a Hungarian poet who had heard me quote some lines of e e cummings to someone, and the sound of it seemed so pure and memorable to me that it came naturally out of the fictional mouth of Sheila Kelly who is kind of an opposite of or counterpart to Cathleen in this story.

Now that the situation was set up — and I still was not consciously aware of the implications of any of this — it was all surface detail driven by deep feeling — the structure began to unfold.

The main character, Volk, whose ancester solved a problem by running from it, goes through a series of actions in an attempt to deliver himself from what he senses as his responsibility for Cathleen. These came to me as they occur in the story, in that order, and I quickly began to sense the rhythm and increasing tempo of their occurrence.

He tries five options:
-psychiatry (twice)
-a magician
-a sexual escape (Sheila)
-flight (his ancestor's option).

All but the last option is punctuated by a visit to the bar where the bartender — I later came to see — was a kind of symbol for Volk of death, the gatekeeper at the underworld, and his daughter a symbol of fertility, Sheela na gig, an exhibitionist goddess adorning certain old Irish churches. I learned that Volk was at a turning point of his existence, where the series of failures that constitute his life are about to be fixed in permanence. He was born, in a sense, of an act of flight, of desertion, and the question is whether he will break or continue the pattern?

I still had no idea what any of this meant, and was troubled by the fact that the story went into a freeze-frame at the end, a TV technique I have always hated. I wanted him to choose, wanted what I felt might be a "true" conclusion, but no matter what I tried, the story would go no further, and finally, I realized that it had already concluded with a kind of epiphany.

Then, looking more closely at what I had written, I began to understand why this series of events had taken place in lonely New York City, where people so often get lost or abandoned, and against the backdrop of Christmas, the celebration of love and caring, why the Christmas tree was a dwarf tree, why it ends with Christmas presents and an embrace — it is in a sense an embrace of Christian responsibility in the big city desert as opposed to the perfunctory symbolism of the embrace which has now become a part of the Mass.

There is no need to take these characters literally as people, although one may if one wishes, or to agonize over precisely what happens to them. The point is that we are responsible for one another, that we are tiny creatures populating the dust of the earth, that our lives are as dust, that we came from dust and will return to dust, yet we have the choice to care, not necessarily to sacrifice ourselves but to care.

So it seems no accident that it ends with a line from T. S. Eliot written at a time when he was struggling toward the embrace of Christianity, a line that came into my mind of its own accord just as Volk was embracing Cathleen and staring over her shoulder at a dust mote.

Except that it *was* an accident — in the sense that I only followed the accumulation of detail, letting them guide me, and the details all came from various, very diverse points of my life, but via the imagination achieved a unity. I can account for virtually every one of them (the overweight psychiatrist is based on a real person although the dialogue between her and Volk just appeared; the magician is based on some readings I had done in Aleister Crowley and in various magical texts; the *New York Post* articles are directly from that catalogue of postmodernism), but I cannot account for why they came together as they did. I did not make the decisions. My imagination did, and the decisions were made over my head and without consulting me, and I was the last to know why, but I did as I was told and actually enjoyed it. I love Christmas in New York, even sad as it often is.

So even if I did not understand what was happening, by giving myself to the process, somehow, something in me — between the hand and the page — brought it all together.

Now the question may be, How do you make that happen? I don't know. But I do know how to make it not happen. By thinking, that is trying to flex the brain rather than calmly reflecting or merely waiting receptively. If I had set out to write a story on such a Christian theme, tried mentally, consciously, to plot and structure it, this story, for what it is worth, would never have been written.

Then how *was* it written? It started with that sentence: "Infinitesimal monsters people the dust." That was from my muse, or from the heat of the process of reading, writing, pondering, worrying until, in a pause, something starts and feels right and lets you follow it, not with the mind so much as by enlisting oneself in the process, trusting the impulse that will hand you the word, the image, the sentence, the movement you need when you need it. And not trying to be larger than the process we work to serve.

AFTERWORD: MAGICK

Finally, dear reader, a magick ritual to infuse those who wish it with artistic prolificity.

I close my eyes, breath deeply, slowly. I tense the muscle of my back, my chest, my latisimus dorsi. I tighten my jaw, my neck, and I focus my concentration to a single sharp beam:

Magick, fly! Infuse her mind, breathe story in his ear, fill her hands with words, fill his mouth with the breath of language, blow with gentle lips into the chemic broil, rising vapors of fiction that take form from all the wealth of human striving of his years, her years, their life, their wisdom.

See!

The clay lifts, footprints in the mud. Across the river, through the dark trees, see the eyes, the fleeting faces, hear the murmur of hidden voices, a gathering...

Stories all around you now, the stuff of life, details, words, visions, inside you, boiling up to be told.

And you must tell them.

All of them.

INDEX

211

Photo by A. Guldbrandsen

ABOUT THE AUTHOR

Thomas E. Kennedy's books include five of fiction (most recently the novel *The Book of Angels* and story collection *Drive, Dive, Dance & Fight*), four of literary criticism (most notably, book-length studies of the short fiction of Andre Dubus and Robert Coover), an essay collection and six anthologies (most recently *Stories & Sources* and *Poems & Sources*, collections of stories and poems with essays by the authors on how they were written).

For ten years he served as International Editor of *Cimarron Review* and currently is an advisory editor of *The Literary Review*, for which he has guest-edited several issues, international editor of *Story Quarterly, Potpourri*, and a contributing editor of the *Pushcart Prize*. His stories, poems, essays, interviews, reviews, and translations from the Danish have appeared in several hundred periodicals and anthologies, including *Kenyon Review, North American Review, Sewanee Review, The Literary Review, New Letters, Glimmer Train, Story Quarterly, Quarterly West, Western Humanities Review, Virginia Quarterly Review, Gettysburg Review, Boulevard, Rosebud*, and others.

His stories have won the *Angoff Award* (1988), *Pushcart Prize* (1990), *O Henry Prize* (1994), and *The European* (1995) and *Gulf Coast* (2000) short story competitions as well as being cited regularly in various award volumes.

Kennedy holds a Ph.D. from Copenhagen University, an MFA from Vermont College of Norwich University, and a BA (summa cum laude) from Fordham University. He has taught in the MFA Program of Vermont College, in the Ploughshares/Emerson College International Writing Seminar in the Netherlands, at Converse College and as visiting writer in many other universities and colleges. He is currently a member of the International Faculty of the Fairleigh Dickenson University MFA Program.

He lives in Denmark with his son and daughter, Daniel and Isabel.

213

WORDCRAFT SPECULATIVE WRITERS SERIES

#1: Prayers of Steel, Misha, 1-877655-00-7 $5
#2: The Magic Deer, Conger Beasley, Jr., 1-877655-01-5 $5
#3: Lifting, Mark Rich, 1-877655-03-1 $7.95
#4: The Liquid Retreats, Todd Mecklem/Jonathan Falk, 1-877655-01-3 (OP)
#5: Oceans of Glass and Fire, Rob Hollis Miller, 1-877655-04-X (OP)
#6: The Seventh Day and After, Don Webb, 1-877655-05-8 (OP)
#7: Pangaea, Denise Dumars, 1-877655-08-2 $7.95 (limited supply)
#8: The Raw Brunettes, Lorraine Schein, 1-877655-12-0 $6.00 (limited supply)
#9: Scherzi, I Believe, Lance Olsen, 1-877655-11-2 (OP)
#10: Ke-Qua-Hawk-As, Misha, 1-877655-13-9 $9.95 (limited supply)
#11: The Eleventh Jagaurundi…, Jessica Amanda Salmonson, 1-877655-14-7, $9.95 (limited supply)
#12: The Blood of Dead Poets, Conger Beasley, Jr., 1-877655-15-5, $9.95
#13: Unreal City, Thomas E. Kennedy, 1-877655-17-1, $11.95
#14: Burnt, Lance Olsen, 1-877655-20-1, $11.95
#15: The Book of Angels, Thomas E. Kennedy, 1-877655-23-6, $12.95
#16: The Din of Celestial Birds, Brian Evenson, 1-877655-24-4, $10.95 (limited supply)
#17: The Explanation & Other Good Advice, Don Webb, 1-877655-25-2, $9.95
#18: The Winter Dance Party Murders, Greg Herriges, 1-877655-26-0, $13.95
#19: Shadow Bones, David Memmott, 1-877655-28-7, $10
#20: Red Spider White Web, Misha, 1-877655-29-5, $12
#21: Splitting, Brian Charles Clark, 1-877655-30-9, $9
#22: Contagion & Other Stories, Brian Evenson, 1-877655-34-1, $11
#23: Freaknest, Lance Olsen, 1-877655-35-X, $12
#24: Smoking Mirror Blues, Ernest Hogan, 1-877655-37-6, $12
#25: Realism & Other Illusions:Essay on the Craft of Fiction, Thomas E. Kennedy, 1-877655-38-4 , $12

See our website for catalog listings
http://www.oregontrail.net/~wordcraft